THE CHRISTIAN MORAL VISION

THE CHURCH'S TEACHING SERIES

Prepared at the request of the Executive Council of the
General Convention of the Episcopal Church

THE
CHRISTIAN
MORAL VISION

Written by Earl H. Brill
with the assistance of a group of
editorial advisors under the direction of the
Church's Teaching Series Committee

1817

HARPER & ROW, PUBLISHERS, SAN FRANCISCO

Cambridge, Hagerstown, New York, Philadelphia
London, Mexico City, São Paulo, Singapore, Sydney

Printed in the United States of America

Library of Congress Cataloging in Publication Data

Brill, Earl H   The Christian moral vision.

(The Church's teaching series; 6)
Includes bibliographical references and index.
1. Christian ethics—Anglican authors.   I. Title.   II. Series.
BJ1251.B74   241'.04'3   79-15499
ISBN 0-8164-0423-2   ISBN 0-8164-2219-2 pbk.

Grateful acknowledgement is made to the 65th General
Convention of the Protestant Episcopal Church for the
use of the material on abortion in chapter 10.

86 87 88 89 90 9 8 7 6 5 4 3 2

Foreword

The series of books published for the most part in the 1950s and known as the Church's Teaching Series has had a profound effect on the life and work of the Episcopal Church during the past twenty years. It is a monumental credit to that original series and to the authors and editors of those volumes that the Church has seen fit to produce a new set of books to be known by the same name. Though the volumes will be different in style and content, the concern for quality education that prompts the issuing of the new series is the same, for the need of Church members for knowledge in areas of scripture, theology, liturgy, history, and ethics is a need that continues from age to age.

I commend this new Church's Teaching Series to all who seek to know the Lord Jesus and to know the great tradition that he has commended to us.

John M. Allin
PRESIDING BISHOP

Introduction

This is one of a series of volumes in the new Church's Teaching Series. The project has been both challenging and exciting. Not only is there a wide variety of opinions regarding the substance of the teaching of the Church, there are also varying and conflicting views with regard to the methods of communicating this teaching to others. That is why we have tried to pay close attention to the various movements within the Church, and to address them. The development of this new series, therefore, has involved hundreds of men and women throughout the Episcopal Church and is offered as one resource among many for the purposes of Christian education.

While it is neither possible nor perhaps even desirable today to produce a definitive series of books setting forth the specific teachings of a particular denomination, we have tried to emphasize the element of continuity between this new series and the old. Continuity, however, implies movement, and we believe that the new series breaks fresh ground in a creative and positive way.

The new series makes modest claims. It speaks not so much *for* the Episcopal Church as *to* it, and not to this Church only but to Christians of other traditions, and to those who wait expectantly at the edge of the Church.

Two words have been in constant use to describe this project from its inception: affirmation and exploration. The writers have affirmed the great insights of the Christian tradition and have also explored new possibilities for the future in the confidence that the future is God's.

Alan Jones
CHAIRMAN OF THE
CHURCH'S TEACHING SERIES
COMMITTEE

THE CHRISTIAN MORAL VISION

Contents

Concl. ←

Preface

All about us today, we hear people lamenting the decline of morality in our time. Old standards are being abandoned. Behavior that once would have brought universal censure—even possibly legal prosecution—now goes unnoticed. Family life is threatened; sexual behavior has undergone revolutionary changes; deceit abounds in business; corruption flourishes in politics. Wherever you look, moral behavior seems to be deteriorating. Some fear that civilization itself is in danger.

At such a time, people look to the church to assert moral leadership. Even people who are not themselves believers seem to expect the church to safeguard the morals of society. The church, according to just about everybody, needs to speak out with moral authority.

The Church and Moral Leadership

The difficulty with this view is that people not only want the church to speak out, but most of them seem to have a very clear idea of what the church ought to say. Most people simply want the church to affirm and support their own moral position over against those other people who think and behave differently.

Genuine moral leadership will resist that sort of demand. Rather than saying what is expected of it, a responsible church will explore its own moral resources and bring them to bear upon contemporary issues. If the church does this faithfully, the results may be quite different from what everyone expects and not to everyone's liking.

This book represents an effort in that direction. It is intended to offer guidance to faithful Christians who are seriously concerned to explore the moral implications of their religious convictions. It does not presume to tell you what you ought to think or do. Rather it offers resources to enable you to make your own responsible choices.

Moral Judgments

You might criticize this open-ended approach on the ground that it can be used by irresponsible people to justify nearly any kind of behavior. That is true, of course, but it is a risk that we have to take. People who really want to do the wrong thing will do it without any help from books like this one. People looking for convenient rationalizations can always find them. A faith grounded in a vision of human freedom and responsibility before God will always incur the risk of being misused.

We are concerned primarily with our own behavior, not that of other people. Our question is "What shall I do?" not "What should another person do?" The distinction is important because it is the difference between morality and moralism, which is the besetting sin of religious people. We tend to make excuses for ourselves, but we are quick to condemn other people. Indeed the chief attraction of clear moral directives is that they can be used to put other people in the wrong. Yet we all have enough to do just to keep our own lives in order without confessing other people's sins.

There is a sound theological principle behind this point of view. God, we are told, both loves us and judges us; in fact, he judges us precisely because he loves us. He has chosen to share with us his function of loving. We are called to love one another as he has loved us. But he has reserved for himself the function of judging, possibly because he knows how much we enjoy it and how poorly we manage to do it. Thus Jesus warned us: "Judge not, that you be not judged" (Mt. 7:1).

There are times, of course, when we have to judge other people. Parents judge their children. Teachers judge their students. Citizens judge their political leaders. We cannot avoid judging others, but if we maintain an awareness of our own frailty and sinfulness, we will judge in a spirit of humility and compassion, not in a spirit of righteous indignation.

Speaking for the Church

There is a peculiar difficulty in writing a moral treatise on behalf of a whole church, especially one as diverse as the Episcopal Church. I have tried to maintain a point of view within the mainstream of Christian thinking, while pointing out areas in which major differences exist. I have tried to be frank in stating my own views, especially where they may seem divergent. I have tried to be faithful to the tradition as I understand it, while recognizing that tradition itself is a live and growing thing.

Terminology

Before entering into this discussion, it might be useful to say a word about the terminology I have used throughout the book. The words *moral* and *ethical* are understood in such different ways that I have opted for one particular way of using them. I use moral and ethical as synonyms, which they originally were—moral coming from a Latin root, ethical from a Greek one. I use these words, not as equivalents for *good* but as a way of identifying that realm of thought and behavior where issues of good and evil, right and wrong, occur.

In this way of speaking, the Christian moral vision is our view of good and evil. A moral choice is one in which issues of right and wrong are at stake. A moral agent is the person who decides for good or evil. Consistent with that usage, I have avoided words like *immoral* and *unethical*. If you find them in the pages that follow, cross them out; they don't belong there.

[handwritten note:] This DISAGREES with Scot/ and Ferrad's point of beginning. For them ethics deals w/ foundation + principles, while morals deal with concrete behavior ... as reflected in their root words.

[handwritten marginal note beside paragraph:] a/

The Plan of the Book

The book is divided into three major parts, with a single concluding chapter. Part 1 develops some ideas about the place of morality in religion and life, the character of the moral agent, the process of making moral choices, and the biblical foundations on which our ethical reflections rest. Part 2 looks at some issues in our private lives, beginning with our personal behavior, then moving out into interpersonal relationships in sex, marriage, and family life.

Part 3 ranges broadly over selected issues in the realm of social, economic, and political life and includes a chapter on medical issues. The concluding chapter considers the role of the church in the moral life.

These distinctions are artificial, of course, for moral issues have a way of cutting across our categories of thought. Sex, for example, is a matter of social concern as well as an issue in our personal lives. At the same time, the largest and most complex political issues can become an occasion for a personal decision, often when we least expect it. The divisions of subject matter are intended to facilitate discussion, not to cut up human existence into neat and tidy pieces.

The Mystery of Evil

You may wonder why, in a book that treats of the moral vision, there is so little discussion of the nature of evil itself. The simple answer is that I really do not understand it. I do not understand why people choose evil over good. I cannot comprehend the depths of human cruelty and viciousness, which are exhibited daily before our eyes. Moral evil is a mystery, just as unfathomable as the mystery of God's own being. It cannot be explained, it can only be reckoned with.

The Christian doctrine of original sin is a way of recognizing the fact of evil in human existence. Even though we cannot understand why it should be, we know that people will choose to do evil knowingly and willfully. We even do it ourselves and do not know exactly why we do it.

Speculation on the nature of evil is pointless in any case. No book can make people good; only the grace of a loving God can do that. All we can do is mark out the choices before us, while looking honestly at their consequences. The mystery of evil lies beyond our vision.

Writing about Moral Issues

I claim no originality for this discussion of the Christian moral vision. In true Anglican fashion, I have cribbed shamelessly from many sources, representing a wide variety of Christian communions, as well as some of the best secular thought of our time. I have cited specific works where that has seemed appropriate, but I have tried to keep notes to a minimum. Readers who want to dig more deeply into any of these matters may refer to the suggested readings at the back of the book.

Finally, I ought to confess that I find it difficult to write engagingly about major moral issues, just as you may find it difficult to read about them. Because they are matters of great importance to people, one does not want to seem to be taking them lightly. But when the writer is trying to be most conscientious, the discussion often gets heavy and even boring. While writing this book I often felt I was suffering from a case of terminal earnestness. So you may find the writing dull and preachy in spots. If so, remember that I tried to avoid it.

Through the centuries, the best of Anglican writing, from John Donne to C. S. Lewis, has managed to steer clear of stuffy solemnity. Anglicans have traditionally found wit, irony, and humor more congenial to their cause. While acknowledging the negativities of life, they have affirmed and celebrated it. And they have been right to do so, for Christianity is, after all, a gospel, a piece of good news. For Christians, the moral life is a joyful response to the promises of a good God. If we can keep that in mind, our moral pilgrimage will become, not a wearisome plodding through this vale of tears but a spirit-filled venture in faith.

Part One

———

A FRAMEWORK
FOR ETHICAL REFLECTION

———

· 1 ·

———

The Nature of the Moral Life

———

What should I do?

How should I live?

How can I know the difference between right and wrong?

What happens if I do the wrong thing?

These are universal questions. In one form or another, they have occurred to people of all societies in every era of history. Everybody wants to be good, as they would define the good. They want to be accepted by God, or to be thought well of by the people who matter to them. They want to be in harmony with the ultimate powers of the universe and with the deepest yearnings of their inner being.

Since right conduct is a universal concern it is not surprising that every culture has some kind of standard by which some actions can be labeled *good* or *right* while others are regarded as *wrong* or *evil*. Most societies have rules that make those standards concrete and coherent so that everyone can understand what is approved and what is disapproved.

Ethics and Religion

The question of right conduct is a universal component of religion. While religion is more than ethics, it always includes ethics. One who believes in a divine order of things will want to live in accordance with the principles of that order, or with the will of the divine being. This sense of duty is expressed in words like *ought, must, should*. Wordsworth

3

referred to duty as the "stern daughter of the voice of God."[1] That sentiment is entirely in accord with the ethical perspective of most major religions.

At the same time, religion sees the moral life as conducive to the well-being of the believer. To live in accord with the divine will is to enjoy satisfaction and fulfillment— contentment if not happiness. For the very basis of the moral life is the conviction that it accords with our deepest nature. To live the good life is to live as we are intended to live. Such a life can only be ultimately satisfying and fulfilling.

Good conduct is not only a universal aspect of religion; it is its most visible aspect. Many people are convinced that morality is all that really matters: "It's not what you believe that counts, but how you live." Matthew Arnold described religion as "morality tinged with emotion."[2] Thomas Paine earlier proclaimed, "To do good is my religion."[3]

If you were to ask the first ten people you saw coming down the street, "What is the essence of Christianity?" they would very likely respond by saying something like:

"You should love your neighbor." Or, "Do unto others as you would have them do unto you."

When people describe someone as "a real Christian," they usually intend a compliment. They mean that the person is a good sort. He loves his neighbor. She keeps her promises. He stays out of trouble.

This tendency to identify a religion by the behavior of its adherents is not limited to Christianity. When people speak of other world religions, they often describe them in behavioral terms as well: Moslems do not drink alcoholic beverages. They can have four wives. Hindus maintain a caste system. They expect a widow to immolate herself on the funeral pyre of her husband. While these statements are more or less accurate, they do not begin to describe the rich complexity of belief, worship, and practice of these great religions.

But conduct is observable. It has consequences. It affects other people. We can see it, evaluate it, and feel concerned about it whether we regard the religion itself as important or not.

Thus many people who do not regard religion as either

important or true are nevertheless concerned with its moral teachings. Because religion provides divine sanctions for morality, they believe that where religion is strong people will be well-behaved. Benjamin Franklin, certainly no orthodox Christian believer, notes in his *Autobiography* that he was always willing to contribute to the building of new houses of worship because they could be counted upon to inspire, promote, or confirm morality.[4]

In the same vein, we often hear, especially from secular sources, that the church ought to assert moral leadership to halt the present decline in morality in our society. The assumption behind this view is that the purpose of religion is to provide social controls. It also assumes that even in a secular society the church has the power to accomplish this goal.

Ethical Inquiry Today

In some societies, moral and ethical issues have been relatively simple because most people agreed on the bases and standards for conduct. When the standards are widely accepted, there is little disagreement on the issues and the society can handle violations of the moral code without much trouble. Even those who are punished will agree that they deserve punishment. In a stable society, those standards seldom change and are seldom challenged.

Needless to say, we do not live in such a period. The whole matter of moral standards is fraught with controversy. This is so for a number of reasons. Most of them have to do with the diversity of ethical views and behavior that coexist side by side in our society.

GLOBAL CONSCIOUSNESS

Throughout this century, we have become more aware of how other people live. As long as a society is isolated, as long as its shared values and standards are the only ones known, people in that society will live out their lives in the assurance that their way is the right way, the only way of being truly human. If they know of other ways of living, they can disregard them because the other people are "barbarians," or "gentiles," or "lesser breeds without the law."

In our era, however, we have learned a great deal about other societies and other ways of living. Our own standards and customs do not always appear superior by comparison. We hear, for example, of tribes that exist without competition or violence. We hear of people whose lives are so free of stress that they regularly live for more than a hundred years. Others seem to live in such close harmony with nature that they feel at one with the elemental powers of the universe.

Of course some of our attitude toward more traditional societies is colored by sentimentality about "the noble savage," but still we have learned to take seriously ways of living different from our own. This is the correct meaning of ethical relativity. Whether we like it or not, we all share it to some extent. That is why it is so difficult for us to assert the absolute truth and superiority of our own traditional morality.

SOCIAL CHANGE

We live in a rapidly changing social environment. Our ways of living change with time; today's behavior can be strikingly different from that of yesterday. In the 1920s, for example, cigarette advertisements never showed women smoking because it was deemed so offensive. Most good religious folk frowned on dancing and card playing. Sunday was strictly observed: no movies or sports events or stores open for business. Today all these things are commonplace and most people would see little evil in them.

But to some those changes may seem to represent a decline in morality, while to others they represent liberation from petty rules. At the same time, other changes can be seen as genuine moral advances. Our society no longer sanctions lynchings, race riots, or racial discrimination. We are coming to have increasing doubts about war as a means of settling international disputes. Capital punishment has been abolished in many places. We have become sensitized to many issues that had not been seen as moral concerns by previous generations.

Our increased knowledge of other kinds of morality combined with these changes in our own moral standards has produced the far-reaching ethical pluralism of our culture. For when new standards emerge, they do not replace those formerly held, except for some people. Others still hold to the old ways, so that new and old continue to exist side by side. Centuries of change in our values and behavior have left us living in something like a moral cafeteria, in which people are (relatively) free to choose their own ethic from a variety of options.

The Christian heritage offers one such option—indeed more than one, because within each Christian community there are many moral options. Christians, like their secular fellow citizens, are affected by the climate of ethical pluralism and changing moral standards. There are Christians, for example, whose moral values have been shaped by the life of the small town and countryside, while others have been formed by city life. The moral commitments of American Christians are likely to be somewhat different from those of African or Asian Christians. This variety of moral styles is not to be regretted, for it merely illustrates the fact that there are many different ways of living out the Christian life. Any discussion of morality in the contemporary church needs to take this fact into consideration.

The Particularity of Christian Morality

Does Christianity offer a distinctive way of life that is different from and superior to all others? Do Christian norms of behavior apply equally to all people, or only to Christians?

Though these two questions sound quite different, they are merely two different ways of raising the same issue: is the Christian life universal or particular? Like many such questions, this one has to be answered both yes and no.

Christians do claim a particular source for their understanding of how they should live. That source is Jesus Christ. For the Christian, God's will for us is revealed in Christ, who is the measure of the quality of life. For the Christian, to be good is to be faithful and obedient to the will of God as

Xian ethics

revealed in Christ. This is the basis of all Christian reflection about what is to be done in any situation.

Christian moral teaching can make no claim upon those who do not share the fundamental convictions upon which it is based. Why be good? Because the God who is revealed in Jesus Christ, the God who loves us and forgives us, the God who saves us from sin and death has called us to his love and service. What is the good? The basic good is love, because God is love, because God has called us to love him and to love one another. These statements are not ethical arguments, they are religious convictions. They will have little persuasive power for people who do not believe in the first place. In this sense, Christian moral teaching is particularistic.

But on the other hand, Christians believe that Christ is Lord, not just Lord of the Church, but Lord of all. Christ is the head of the whole human race, as Anglican theologian F. D. Maurice put it.[5] God's will is not just for Christians, but for all humankind; his love embraces all. Love is not just a particularistic demand upon Christian believers; it is the fundamental underlying principle of unity in all creation.

Love is the highest good, then, not just for Christians but for all people. Justice is the proper goal of our community life, no matter what we may believe. Hence Christians believe that what we are called to be and do is what God wants all people everywhere to be and do. Christian teaching that is grounded in the principles of love and justice can be supported by others outside the community of faith on moral, if not religious, grounds. In this sense, Christian moral teaching can claim to be universal.

This has to be said with a great deal of care, however, because Christians have in the past been tempted to impose their particular ethical standards upon other people, even using the civil law for that purpose. Thus when most American Protestants believed that one should neither work nor play on the Lord's Day, they sponsored legislation which forced businesses to remain closed on Sunday. These laws are only now disappearing from the books as fewer and fewer people take them seriously. Nevertheless they represent one instance of the tendency of religious people to force others to conform to their standards even though those others may not share their faith.

We Christians need to recognize the right of other people to oppose our ethical views, even those views which we think should commend themselves to all people. We, like most people in the world today, live in an ethically pluralistic culture. In such a society, we can properly claim the right to follow our own moral convictions, but we must at the same time accord that right to those of other persuasions. This may seem obvious when the issue is something peripheral like Sunday closing laws, but it becomes more difficult to concede when matters of greater significance are involved, as we shall see later. _e.g. abortion_

While we have no right to coerce others into behaving in ways we regard as right and good, we do have the right to try to persuade others to accept our views. And by the same token, we owe others the right to a fair hearing of their own views. We might, on occasion, actually be persuaded that we were wrong, or at least that the contrary view proceeds from valid principles.

Perhaps a useful guideline in such situations is the recognition that if an ethical position truly represents a universally valid principle, then it will commend itself to some non-Christians on rational grounds. If Christians find themselves isolated in their advocacy of a moral position, it may be that the entire society has lapsed into an inhuman barbarism. It is more likely, however, that the Christians are merely in error.

In actuality, Christians seldom find themselves in complete agreement against the whole outside world on any moral issue. Most often we find as many differences within the Christian community as there are differences between Christians and non-Christians. Too many other nontheological factors enter into our ethical reflections to enable all Christians to _sad!_ speak with one united voice.

The Anglican Ethical Perspective

This book is intended to be read by members of the Protestant Episcopal Church in the United States of America, a church which stands within the theological and ethical tradition of Anglicanism. In what sense can it claim to be Anglican in its perspective? It is difficult to distinguish the ethical teachings of Anglicanism from those of the Presbyterian Church or the Roman Catholic Church. Indeed, even within the Episcopal Church there are sharp differences in our views of Christian morality.

Nevertheless I am convinced that we can identify a characteristic Anglican viewpoint that informs our treatment of ethical concerns. It does not produce for us a uniform code of conduct, but it does suggest how we might approach these matters and what resources we might draw upon.

CHRISTIAN ANTHROPOLOGY

HUMAN FREEDOM AND HUMAN SINFULNESS

The first consideration in developing an Anglican perspective is what would once have been called a "Christian anthropology," a doctrine that establishes the moral status of humanity. It seeks to answer the perennial question, "Are we inherently good or evil?"

Anglicans would respond to this question by pointing to the biblical declaration that God has made us in his own image. We have been endowed by God with the capacity for freedom, for making our own moral choices. We can choose to think, to believe, to act as we wish. We can choose our own loyalties. We can choose whom or what we shall serve.

Lifree moral agents in God's image

But because we are free, we are also capable of misusing our freedom. We can choose evil as well as good. We can choose to rebel as well as to obey. What is more, experience teaches that we will do just that. When Christians refer to the doctrine of original sin, they mean to say that, when offered a choice, we will most likely choose the evil over the good.

We do that because we see the world through our own small porthole. We put ourselves into first place. We manipulate and exploit others. And worst of all, we hide from ourselves the truth about our evil inclinations. Our sinfulness subverts all our attempts to achieve moral perfection, all our movements to build a better world. If we understand the full

range and power of human sinfulness, we can never be op-
timistic about human possibilities for goodness.

That is why the center of Christianity is not the moral law
but the Gospel: the proclamation that in Christ, God has
provided the Saviour who has done for us what we cannot do
for ourselves. He has died for our sins and has been raised
from the dead for our salvation. The cross is the symbol of the
terrifying power of human sinfulness. The risen Lord is the
sign of God's grace and power that overcomes sin and death.
Because Christ died and rose again, we are free. And for
Christians, the moral life is our sacrifice of praise and
thanksgiving to God for that salvation which is given to us.

Christians of all persuasions would agree with this outline
of the Gospel message, but they would differ in their emphasis upon one or another aspect. The major theologians of
the Reformation, Luther and Calvin especially, were most
impressed by the depth of human sinfulness. Concerned to
counter the power of human pride, they insisted that humankind can do no good thing, for in our fall from grace the
image of God in us was obliterated.

Though Anglicans were early infected with Calvinistic pes-
simism, as the Thirty-nine Articles of Religion testify, they
never carried the idea of human depravity to such extremes.
Anglican thinkers insisted on maintaining the essential
goodness of God's creation. They denied that the fall had
obliterated the image of God in us, asserting instead that we
retain the capacity to respond to the grace of God.

The most recent revision of the Book of Common Prayer
implies this view because it has eliminated from the General
Confession the phrase, ". . . and there is no health in us."
For that statement seemed to deny the persistence of God's
image in us. Anglicans, then, believe that though sin is an
undeniable fact which can be overcome only by God's grace
and forgiveness, nevertheless God has not totally absented
himself from the life of sinful humanity.

The Anglican view of humanity, then, is two-sided. It recognizes the fact of sinfulness, but denies that this is the last
word to be said. The image of God makes our freedom opera-

tive, even though it is limited and distorted by sin. We have the capacity for both good and evil; therefore we have responsibility for our own moral choices. And most important of all, we have available to us the grace and forgiveness of God when we fail and repent of our evil ways.

SOURCES OF AUTHORITY
FOR ETHICAL REFLECTION

When Anglicans are asked to identify the authority by which they make theological or ethical pronouncements, they appeal to three sources: Scripture, tradition, and reason.

All Christians agree that the Bible is our central authority for both theology and ethics. In it the Word of God is disclosed to us through his relationship with Israel, in the law and the prophets, but preeminently in the person and work of Jesus Christ. But Anglicans have seldom treated the Bible in a literalistic manner.

Richard Hooker, for example, disputed Puritan interpretations of doctrine late in the sixteenth century by pointing out that, while Holy Scripture does contain all that is necessary to salvation, not all the laws of Scripture are to be understood as literally binding for all time. Some, he noted, are obscure in meaning; others are manifestly intended for particular times and places, not forever. Christians in every age must judge to what extent a passage of Scripture is intended to apply to their own situation.[6]

In contrast with most Protestants, Anglicans have always accorded a significant place to tradition as an authority for Christian life and thought. We value tradition because we recognize that the Christian enterprise has been around for a long time and has compiled a significant body of experience in relating the Gospel to life. Whatever the issue facing us, we can be sure that Christians at other times and places have faced something similar. We have much to learn from them.

But tradition is not always a reliable guide, for it is not always clear that standards and beliefs which were right and just at some other point in history would be equally valid for our own situation. We do learn from history. But still, new occasions do teach new duties. A slavish devotion to tradition can be for us an irresponsible evasion of our own moral responsibilities. Thus we should respect tradition without worshiping it or absolutizing its demands.

Because Anglicans respect tradition, we are relatively slow to change. We tend to hold onto old ways, sometimes far too long. But occasionally those older views come back into style and then the traditionalist begins to look like the avant garde.

Finally, Anglicans have always placed a high value on the use of reason, in keeping with the view that sinful human beings still retain the image of God which enables them to exercise their reason responsibly. Reason is the instrument which we bring to bear upon our examination of both Scripture and tradition in order to make judgments as to how they should inform our own moral decisions. Reason enables us to think our way through moral perplexities. It is through this use of reason that we love the Lord "with all our mind."

This respect for human reason has enabled Anglicans to accept and make use of the findings of modern biblical scholarship without resorting to doctrinal upheavals and heresy trials. It has also led us to value the intellectual contributions of thinking people in various areas of secular thought. The social and behavioral sciences, for example, throw significant light on ethical issues. Because we respect these achievements, we can incorporate them into our moral and ethical reflections.

These two factors, our commitment to human freedom and our confidence in human reason, lead us to place the burden of moral choice upon the person who is confronted by the decision. Anglicanism is not given to rules—either commands or prohibitions. It tends to be permissive rather than legalistic, not because ethical issues are unimportant but because each person is unique, as is each moral situation. This, no doubt, is why there is so much diversity in the moral commitments of Episcopalians. It is also why we are able to respect and care for one another in the midst of that diversity.

· 2 ·

Character and Moral Vision

When we think about the moral life, we tend to think about issues: Is it ever right to tell a lie? Should capital punishment be abolished? What should be our attitude toward euthanasia?

No matter what the issue, however, moral choices are made by persons. It becomes crucial, then, to understand the place of the person in our consideration of Christian behavior. What is moral character? How is it shaped and developed? How does Christian faith affect character?

The Significance of Character

Character is the word that we use to describe the ethical core of a person. If we know a person's character, we know something about how that person is likely to act in a given situation. We even describe a person's actions as being in "character" or out of "character."

Our Christian heritage places more emphasis on character than on issues. Indeed, the very center of our faith is a person rather than an idea. Even before the coming of Christ ancient Israel recognized the significance of persons as bearers and revealers of the will of God for his people. Thus the prophets were seen as those called to declare the Word which God had disclosed to them in visions. Israel looked back to the great heroes of their past as exemplars of who they were and what they ought to be. Abraham, Isaac, and Jacob were revered as the patriarchs who had originally received the promises of

14

an interesting question for reflection: what exactly is the "character" of each of the important O.T. characters?

God. Moses was remembered and celebrated as the bringer of the law. David the King was honored as the special favorite of God because of his loyalty and faith.

In Psalms and Proverbs, the moral exemplar is "the righteous," who do not stand in the way of sinners, nor sit in the seat of scoffers (Ps. 1:1). They give liberally (Ps. 37:26); their mouth brings forth wisdom (Pr. 10:31); their thoughts are just (Pr. 12:5).

The righteous love the law of the Lord and meditate upon it day and night (Ps. 1:2). Therefore they understand what the law requires and are moved to do that which the Lord commands. In our language, we would say that the righteous are formed and shaped by the law.

JESUS AS MORAL MODEL

In the New Testament, the personal character of the moral life is dramatized in the person and work of Jesus Christ. Indeed, for the Christian, the new life can be described as being *in* Christ. During the past generation, the matter of Christian discipleship has been overshadowed by an emphasis on "justification by faith alone." There is no real contradiction between the two concepts. It might be useful, therefore, to look at the meaning of the Christian life as "the imitation of Christ" or "following Christ."

For the Christian, Jesus personifies the moral life. He teaches by what he is and does as well as by what he says. In saying this, we have to separate out the core of his moral character from the accidents of his personal history. The fact that he never married, for example, should not suggest to us that married life is inferior. The fact that, so far as we know, he engaged in no gainful employment should not lead us to repudiate the working life. His rejection of home, family, and career were his peculiar vocation, in keeping with his perception of the imminence of the kingdom of God and his total commitment to his task of proclaiming that kingdom and of bringing it into being in his person.

We come much closer to the center of Jesus' moral character when we perceive the human compassion that characterized his total ministry. He taught the crowds that followed him. He fed the hungry multitudes in the wilderness. He healed the sick. There is no record in the New Testament of anyone coming to Jesus with a burden who did not receive all the help that Jesus could give. He even allowed people's cares to reshape his own ministry. When asked for help by a Canaanite woman, for example, he brushed her off with the comment, "I was sent only to the lost sheep of the house of Israel." But when she persisted, he did what she had asked, commending her great faith (Mt. 15:22–28).

Though love was at the center of his moral character, Jesus was nonetheless deeply committed to the cause of righteousness. It figures largely in his teaching; it is evidenced most spectacularly in his cleansing of the Temple. He drove the moneychangers out of his father's house of prayer because, as he said, "You make it a den of robbers" (Mt. 21:13).

But it is in his willing acceptance of the cross that Jesus manifests his deepest moral commitment. The act of willing surrender of his life to the pain and suffering of crucifixion declares, in a way that no mere words could convey, that the center of his life is love for all: sinners and righteous alike. Jesus' willingness to face suffering and death, his refusal to avoid the pain and degradation of his crucifixion, constituted a kind of divine humility that calls for imitation by the Christian, as Paul puts it:

> Have this mind among yourselves, which you have in Christ Jesus, who, though he was in the form of God, did not count equality with God a thing to be grasped, but emptied himself, taking the form of a servant, being born in the likeness of men. And being found in human form he humbled himself and became obedient unto death, even death on a cross (Phil. 2:5–8).

Our consideration of Christian moral character has to take into account what it means to be a follower of this Jesus who lived a life of compassion and died a death of sacrificial love.

Some would not agree with the use of this word. I'm not sure.

In fact, it can be argued that compassion and the cause of righteousness are 2 aspects of his love for all, as is sacrifice.

The Effect of Genetics on Moral Character

What are the ingredients of moral character? What goes into making us what we are? How are we affected by what we believe? These questions are difficult to answer because many factors are involved. Nevertheless, it can be helpful to look at some of the more prominent forces so that we can better understand them and thereby attain more control over our own moral life.

Behavioral scientists have long disputed the question whether we are more influenced by heredity or environment. Obviously both have some impact, although the effect of each will differ remarkably in different people. To look at heredity first, we can say with some assurance that our genetic endowment sets some outer limits to what we can achieve. Our native intelligence is given to us, although we can make better or worse use of it through education and effort. Our physical constitution is also given, although we can improve our physical condition. I rather doubt that moral traits are inherited, although our genetic endowment may mark out the areas of our more likely moral achievements and hazards.

A strong, healthy, and vigorous person, for example, may find the virtues of courage and endurance to be congenial, but may be tempted to be aggressive and even cruel. A weaker person may find it easy to be kind and inoffensive but be prone to sins of omission, not doing the kind or generous thing when given the opportunity. Neither personality structure is morally superior, but each may shape the direction of that person's moral life.

But on the other hand, those predictable events may not come to pass at all. For despite what the proponents of heredity say, it is also true that people have the capacity to accomplish deeds that their genetic inheritance would seem to render unlikely. That weak person may make his very weakness the center of moral concern, striving to overcome it and thereby becoming more courageous, more generous, more enduring than the person whose natural dispositions would make those virtues easiest to achieve. Even though we may know people very well, we can seldom tell whether their character is a product of their genetic inheritance or whether it constitutes a transcending of that inheritance.

The Effect of Society on Moral Character

While the effect of genetic inheritance on moral character is difficult to assess, the effect of our social environment is rather obvious. Society provides the context in which moral development takes place. It feeds us the ideas, the attitudes, and the values that go into making us moral agents.

In our society, for example, nearly all would agree that individuals ought to be permitted to marry whom they choose. We regard love and affection as the very root of the marriage relationship. The idea that marriages should be arranged by third parties strikes us as barbaric and wrong.

Yet we know that, in other times and places, marriage was regarded as an alliance of families in which the personal wishes of the couple counted for very little. People were often betrothed as children, without even knowing their future mate. We are inclined to regard those practices as morally inferior, but our view of the matter is largely determined by our social environment. Any alternative to choosing your own mate in marriage is, as we would say, unthinkable.

We do not arrive at that view independently. Indeed we do not "arrive" at that view at all. We rather assume it because it is the only view we know. It "fits" into our larger system of values: the dignity of the individual, the right of persons to make their own choices about the things that matter most to them, the conviction that marriage is grounded in love. All of these values, attitudes, and perceptions are transmitted to us by our society.

As we go through life, we continue to absorb signals from society. The *dos* and *don'ts* that we hear as children let us know what sort of behavior is legitimate and what is not. "You don't take someone else's toy without permission"— which teaches us something about the sanctity of private property. Grades and report cards teach us to be competitive.

Those signals shape our behavior, and our behavior in turn

Socialization;

helps to reinforce those factors in society. That is, our behavior becomes part of the signal system by which those same values are communicated to others. Thus we are acted upon by society, but we also act upon society by the way we behave.

This process, which social scientists call "socialization," insures that each person who grows up in a society will fit into that society as an adult. Though some may try to resist the socialization process, their capacity to do so is rather limited.

Resist

A few years ago, it was common for young people to express contempt for this process. Many proclaimed that we were all being "programed" by the schools and colleges, the big corporations, and the government, so that we would fit quietly and easily into "the system." They were right, of course, but what they saw as unwarranted interference with personal freedom was merely the inevitable process by which all societies insure their continuance. Indeed, the protest itself was ironic proof that these young people had been socialized by the American values of freedom, autonomy, and self-reliance which provided the ideological basis for their protest.

We cannot escape socialization. But on the other hand, socialization is a rather haphazard process that never fully succeeds. We internalize some values but not others. We accept some things wholeheartedly, some only diffidently, some not at all. The process works just a bit differently for each person, which is why, even in the same society, people will vary widely in their attitudes, beliefs, and values. For this reason, it is not accurate to say that society "determines" who we are and what we do. It is more useful to speak of "conditioning." Human freedom is limited by the social context, but not abolished by it.

social context is a limitation

CONSCIOUSNESS-RAISING

Part of the task of ethical reflection is to become more aware of how we are affected by our social context. As long as these influences are unknown to us, we are subject to them because we take them for granted. It is only when social and cultural influences are brought to the level of awareness that we can make any choice as to whether we will accept them or resist them.

The term *consciousness-raising* describes this process of bringing to awareness the forces that influence our lives. We often accept unpleasant conditions because we believe, often without thinking, that they are justifiable or inevitable. But once we recognize something as evil and come to believe that it can be changed, then we are likely to try to make the needed change.

A current example of this process can be found in the women's movement, which has begun to alter the place of women in our society. Not all women have been programed into marriage and child-rearing, but that has been the standard expectation for most women. Women sometimes had to pay a heavy price to serve home and family. Many gave up budding careers for the sake of their families. Many gave themselves to housekeeping and child-rearing tasks even though they found that those tasks were burdensome and uncongenial—and that they might be quite unsuited to them. But those negativities were generally accepted because they were seen as both legitimate and necessary. If a woman felt anger about her lot, she tended to feel guilty about her anger. Consequently, few women were inspired to change their situation.

The women's movement developed as women began to reflect upon their social role and the way in which society's expectations affected their lives. In many places, groups of women would come together to share their experiences in an effort to understand what had been happening to them. As a result of those discussions, many women have concluded that society's standard expectations are neither inevitable nor legitimate. In various ways they have been making decisions about their lives that are different from what they would otherwise have done.

We are beginning to see the consequences of those choices. More women now go into the job market with every intention of establishing a career. Various combinations of home and career are being tried out. In many families, husband and wife share household duties to an extent almost unknown in previous generations. It is too soon to evaluate these changes, but enough has happened to show us what can result when people become conscious of how their society affects them and then decide to do something to change their condition.

We can make responsible choices only if we know what is going on, what is happening to us. We gain some leverage on the social process only if we know what it is. We can criticize the values of society only if we are conscious of them and how they affect people. Once we are aware of what is going on, we can make a conscientious decision to affirm or resist. That decision is our ethical opportunity.

The Effect of Belief on Moral Character

Our society tends to downgrade belief as a component of moral behavior. "It's not what you believe, but how you live that counts." But that expression ignores the fact that what we believe can have a profound effect on how we live.

A terrorist, acting in the belief that he is bringing about a new and more just social order, may kill and destroy without feeling any sense of guilt. He may even give his life for the cause, perhaps in an event that outsiders would consider trivial and meaningless—the attempted assassination of a minor official, for instance. I once heard a lawyer say that the law is a great game, the object of which is to get away with as much as you can. If you get caught, well, you just pay the penalty. I have no doubt that this belief affected the way he practiced his profession.

Of course our beliefs affect our conduct. Some would go further and claim that our conduct inevitably discloses our beliefs. You may say that you believe it is wrong to steal. But if you are a worker who steals tools from the job, or if you cheat on your tax returns, then you are demonstrating that you really believe that stealing is not so very wrong, no matter what you may say to the contrary. If you want to discover what someone really believes, do not ask them; just observe their behavior. Conduct is the best clue to a person's real beliefs.

There is much truth to this point of view. It certainly has logic on its side. But that is just the trouble. We humans are not always that logical. The logical view has no place in it for the complexities and contradictions of human nature. A person can honestly believe in something but still may betray those beliefs at the decisive moment.

The belief may be held in a conventional way, without much real conviction behind it. For example: "everybody knows" it is wrong to steal. Or the person may simply be unaware that he is contradicting his own beliefs; he may not have put the belief together with the behavior. Americans have long expressed their belief in human equality while at the same time maintaining a system of legal separation of the races and economic discrimination against black people. The contradiction may be pushed out of our consciousness, or we may rationalize it as a necessary evil.

When our behavior contradicts our beliefs, the beliefs may be real enough, but we may be out of touch with them. In the Christian vocabulary, this is what we mean by sin. Paul expressed the dilemma most forcefully in his Epistle to the Romans:

> I do not understand my own actions. For I do not do what I want, but I do the very thing I hate. Now if I do what I do not want, I agree that the law is good. So then it is no longer I that do it, but sin which dwells within me (7:15–17).

So belief shapes behavior, yet behavior often contradicts belief. And to further complicate the matter, it is also true that behavior shapes belief. Just as faith leads us to worship, so worship can evoke and enliven faith. If you have always lived in an authoritarian society, you may believe that only the imposition of authority makes society possible. But if you then experience life in an open society, you may learn to value individual liberty and the right to make your own choices. Your experience will have reshaped your beliefs about society.

In our own time, we have discovered something of the

② a good expression of Communist society, AND its fears

connection between belief and behavior as the relationship of the races has begun to change. There is no doubt that racial prejudice against black people has fostered discrimination and exploitation. But we have also learned that the reverse is true as well: prejudice is to some extent a product of discrimination.

As long as the races were separated, few white people had any experience of black people except as servants or menials. It was easy for them to regard all black people as stupid or lazy. But as the walls of racial prejudice have begun to break down, as people of all races have begun to live and work together, their mutual stereotypes have begun to break down. White people see black professionals with as much talent and competence as themselves. They see in black families the same concern for raising children, providing for their education, providing for their own declining years. It turns out that there is as much diversity within the races as between them.

As a result of these new experiences, white people simply can no longer hold to their convenient beliefs about black inferiority. New beliefs have been brought about by new forms of behavior.

The relationship between belief and behavior is too complex to be summed up in trite little phrases. Yet each of the phrases is true to some extent. No one of them can convey the whole truth. 'It's not what you believe, but how you live that counts." "Your beliefs shape your conduct." "What you do is what you believe." "Your conduct shapes your beliefs."

To understand the Christian moral vision, then, we have to look at the nature of our convictions as well as the actions related to them. Only then can we see how convictions and actions affect each other and how either may be changed.

Models of the Moral Self

The discussion of what it means to be a moral agent is often confused by the fact that people have very different ways of understanding the moral self. H. Richard Niebuhr contributed to the clarity of these discussions by proposing several

H. Richard Niebuhr

different models of the moral self.[1] These models can help us to identify our own assumptions when we think about moral character and decision-making.

MAN-THE-CITIZEN

The oldest and most widely used image of the moral agent is the citizen, which sees the moral actor as one who lives under law and responds ethically out of a concern to do one's duty. Duty becomes the highest good, obedience the cardinal virtue, disobedience the chief sin. This image is rooted in the common experience of humanity: we grow up in the midst of rules. The concern to do what is right is built into us early in our lives.

It is easy to see how deeply this image is embedded in the Christian tradition. As we have already seen, the law is at the center of the moral life in the Old Testament. For ancient Israel, disobedience is the ultimate offense against the Lord of the covenant. It is no wonder then that Christians have traditionally seen the moral life as one of duty under the law.

MAN-THE-MAKER

This model sees the moral agent as the one who makes, controls, fabricates the self. The self strives toward a goal or ideal: love, or truth, or justice, or the good life. Acts are judged as good or evil to the extent to which they lead the person toward or away from the goal. Sin, rather than being a transgression of the law, is seen as "missing the mark" which is the literal meaning of the Greek word for sin.

Ethical idealism is one secular version of this model of the moral life, but there are Christian versions as well. The ideas of Christian perfection, sanctification, and growth toward salvation are all built upon the assumption that the ethical acts characteristic of people are pointed toward some goal or purpose. A goal-oriented ethic tests the goodness of specific acts by asking whether they move us toward the goal we have already accepted.

MAN-THE-ANSWERER

This is the model to which Niebuhr himself was commit-
ted. It assumes that our moral choices are responses to actions *i.e.,*
that have already been taken by ourselves or others. We make *social*
context
most of our moral decisions in situations where we have only
a limited number of options. Just as a nation's history can
best be understood by seeing the challenges it has had to
meet, so the moral life of an individual can best be understood in terms of that person's responses to the available
choices.

Niebuhr illustrates this concept by referring to the ethics of
suffering, a condition of life which we have not willed, but to
which we must respond. We all know of people who have
been broken by suffering; we know of others who have been
purified and strengthened by it. The difference suggests that
one's response to suffering is more significant morally than
the suffering itself. When we speak of suffering as "building
character," therefore, we do not place a value on the suffer-*or*
ing, we are paying tribute to the heroism with which the
sufferer has responded.

In order to make the fitting response, Niebuhr notes, we
have to be able to interpret the action upon us. Even children
are less affected by the commands of their parents than by
their own interpretation of the attitudes behind the commands. We respond to other people on the basis of our interpretation of the meaning of their actions toward us.

Take the case of a woman who is driving alone at night. She
notices that another car has been behind her for some time.
Whenever she turns, the other car turns. What does it mean?
If she concludes that it means she is being followed, she will
be alarmed. She will take evasive action, or head for the
nearest police station. But if she assumes that the other driver
is merely heading to a destination near her own, she will not
be alarmed and will take no action. In either case, the action
upon her is the same. Her interpretation will govern her response.

For man-the-citizen, the moral question is "What is right?"
For man-the-maker, the question is "What is good?" For

*Whereas, if we focus on the suffering itself, we are
liable to come up with some such statement as
"God sent the suffering in order to build our character."*

man-the-answerer, it is "What is fitting?" Niebuhr observes that this is what Aristotle meant when he described the "mean" which constitutes virtue: "To feel fear, confidence, appetite, anger, and pity 'at the right times, with reference to the right objects, toward the right people, with the right motive and in the right way, is what is intermediate and best.'"[2]

To reach a decision as to "What is fitting," it is first necessary to ask, "What is going on?" Man-the-answerer attempts to piece together as much information as possible about the situation before deciding what needs to be done. To be sure, knowledge alone does not guarantee a fitting response, but a fully responsible choice demands the best information available.

This ethic of what Niebuhr calls "the responsible self" is religiously neutral. But put into the context of Christian faith, which is where Niebuhr puts it, it can offer us a way of making moral choices, bringing to bear on the immediate situation the values and commitments of our Christian heritage. We will be referring to this process in our discussion of decision-making and in later chapters as well.

A Theory of Moral Development

How do people grow morally? What kinds of experience might help them grow?

Psychologist Lawrence Kohlberg has proposed a theory of moral development based on the reasons people give for behaving in particular ways.[3] He identifies three levels of moral development, each level consisting of two stages—a total of six stages of development.

The lowest level, characteristic of children, Kohlberg calls preconventional because behavior is judged on the basis of what is good for the self. At the first stage, the punishment/ obedience orientation, goodness and badness are related to the physical consequences of an act. A bad act is one that brings punishment. The child moves to the second stage, the instrumental/relativist orientation, when he discovers that if he does things for others, they will do things for him. When children learn to share toys, for example, they have entered this second stage.

Young people move into the conventional level as they begin to identify with something larger than the self, namely society. Kohlberg calls stage three the good boy/nice girl orientation because good behavior is seen as that which helps others and is approved by them. The reward is the good feeling that comes from knowing you have pleased those who are important to you.

The next stage, the law-and-order orientation, provides the basis for a larger loyalty than the group. The principle of order itself becomes the major value because it is the foundation for all other rights and privileges. Since every transgression weakens respect for the law, it is wrong to break the law even in a good cause.

As adults come to maturity, they may move to what Kohlberg calls the postconventional level of moral autonomy. At this level, the individual takes responsibility for deciding what society ought to expect, what the rules ought to be. Through principled thinking, the moral agent seeks to discover and to live by the basic values from which all laws are derived.

At the postconventional level, Kohlberg identifies a fifth stage of development, the social contract/legalistic orientation which affirms the values of one's own society while recognizing the relativity of those values. The law is legitimate but not absolute; laws should be upheld insofar as they promote the common good, but if they are unjust they should be changed.

At the final stage, the individual is committed to universal ethical principles such as justice, equality of human rights, and respect for the dignity of each person. Among these universal principles, Kohlberg includes Jesus' statement of the Golden Rule: ". . . whatever you wish that men would do to you, do so to them" (Mt. 7:12). He also includes Immanuel Kant's categorical imperative: "So act that the maxim of your will could always hold at the same time as the principle of a universal legislation."[4]

Kohlberg maintains that the individual has to move through each stage in order to reach the next one. The movement takes place when the reasoning of the current stage proves inadequate for dealing with a moral dilemma. A young person caught in the conflicting demands of differing groups, for example, might be led to develop a sense of loyalty to the principle of law and order as a way of determining which group has the most legitimate claim.

The theory is neater and tidier than real life, to be sure, but it conforms generally to what we know about moral development. Though not grounded in a Christian perspective, Kohlberg's theory supports the Christian conviction that egoism is a lower level of development than is a commitment to universal principles. While Kohlberg has much to say about equality and justice, the Christian would want to say more about love, which we would regard as the highest ethical norm.

Christians, moreover, would want to extend the idea of development beyond autonomy, for we understand the highest form of freedom to be a freely accepted commitment to God and his purposes. Faith includes loyalty, the free acceptance of a discipline that takes the form of obedience, as in the prayer that reads, ". . . to serve you is perfect freedom" (the new Prayer Book, p. 99).

Despite these limitations, the Kohlberg theory can help us to understand the nature of moral development and can suggest some ways for the church to aid in the moral formation of its members. It could serve as the basis for a program of moral education in the local congregation.

VARIETIES OF MORAL ATTITUDE

Not only do people vary in their ethical commitments and their moral development, they also differ in their basic attitude toward the moral life. One easily observable distinction is that between the active and the passive forms of moral response.

The active person conceives of the moral life as doing good. This may take the form of helping others, engaging in social or political movements, exhibiting the virtues of courage and compassion. For the active person, it is important to be involved and concerned.

There are hazards in moral activism. The activist, in doing much, may do the wrong thing—taking risks, rushing in before calculating the cost. Such a person may do damage by doing good.

The passive moral stance is more traditional and perhaps more respectable. The passive style conceives of morality as doing no wrong, staying out of trouble, keeping one's self "unstained by the world" (Jas. 1:27). Thus good people are defined by what they do not do. Conventional American Protestant morality—no smoking, no drinking, no dancing—was this kind of morality.

Passive morality is cautious, safe, but not very exciting or generous. Its hazards are equally obvious. Its slogan: "If you don't do anything, you can't do anything wrong," is true enough. But it is also true that you can do nothing good or noble. If you take no risks, you accomplish nothing. If you guard your moral purity, you will miss many opportunities to show love, to strive for justice. Passive types can become totally preoccupied with their own moral status and fail to see human need right before their eyes.

Both moral attitudes are legitimate, though both have their hazards. The General Confession recognizes both when it asks the passive type to confess, "We have left undone those things which we ought to have done," while the active type confesses, "We have done those things which we ought not to have done." Our judgment of other peoples' moral failures often stems from the fact that active types find it easy to condemn the passive, and vice versa.

It may well be that our characteristic moral stance has more to do with our temperament than with our convictions. It may be a part of our total personality that we can do little to change. But we can at least be aware of what category we normally fall into, so that we can guard against the hazards of that particular style. At the same time, we can recognize and affirm those others whose moral style is different from our own.

In parts 2 and 3, we will be looking at issues rather than persons. It is important to keep in mind, however, that the character of the person is a key element in the moral equation. The attitudes and values, the convictions and perceptions that the person brings to the situation will shape their response to that situation. Likewise, the stage of the person's moral development and their characteristic moral attitude will have a significant impact.

We need to know these things about ourselves so that we are able to be fully responsible in making our own decisions. We need to understand how these factors may lead other persons, quite legitimately, to make decisions very different from those we would make in similar circumstances. We can never hope to fully understand our neighbors, their total situation, or even ourselves. That is why we make our moral choices in fear and trembling, calling upon the Lord to forgive the shortcomings that will inevitably be a part of what we decide to do.

· 3 ·

Making Ethical Decisions

Ethics, for most of us, is a matter of making decisions. When we think about the moral life, we normally do not think of the long, steady process of developing moral character; we think, rather, of "What shall I do in this situation?"

Ethical decision-making is difficult to discuss because Christians use different methods of making moral choices. In this chapter, I would like to discuss some of these methods: what they involve, how they function, and what makes them more or less helpful. These positions will be stated in somewhat oversimplified form as an aid to clarity, though the reader will recognize that actual decision-making can be far more complicated in real situations where any number of factors have to be considered.

In thinking our way through a moral dilemma, we often move from one of these approaches to another, without even being aware of the fact. One outcome of this discussion, therefore, might be that we will become more conscious of the bases on which we make our decisions. We can then become more intentional about how we will make decisions in the future.

"Rule Deontology"

Rule Morality   *"Law"* α

Our first thought about morality is that it means "keeping the rules." Christians are often thought of simply as people who do (or do not do) certain things. Different groups of Christians are identified with the rules they are presumed to fol-

also, Act deontology

low. Thus everybody knows that Methodists do not drink alcoholic beverages; that stricter churches like the Nazarenes even frown on drinking coffee. Quakers are pacifists. The Amish disapprove of automobiles. Roman Catholics are opposed to contraception. Most all Christians would agree that you should not tell lies; that you should always keep the law.

There are some obvious advantages to rules. They offer clear guidelines. When you know the rules, you know when you are right and when you are wrong; there is no moral ambiguity to worry about. The disadvantages are equally obvious. Rules offer no flexibility to enable people to cope with new or unusual situations. They always have to be overhauled as new conditions emerge. Rules can produce evil as well as good.

The philosopher Immanuel Kant is generally regarded as the most eloquent spokesman for the absolute validity of the moral rule. Kant would not even admit the legitimacy of telling a lie to save a life. Suppose a man setting out to kill someone comes to your door looking for his intended victim who is hiding inside. He asks you if his enemy is there. According to Kant, you are obligated to tell him the truth, even though it costs the victim his life. Kant's reason is that telling the truth is the only basis for the trust and mutuality which make society possible. Once we begin to excuse lapses from the truth, all of society is in peril.[1]

Most of us could agree with Kant's concern for safeguarding society by preserving the integrity of our word, but we would not agree that a person should betray a victim to a murderer. In this example, we have a conflict of several rules. A second rule would be: one should always act so as to protect human life. That rule would seem, in this case, to override the duty to tell the truth.

Extreme as it is, this example suggests to us a major difficulty with rule morality. It offers no guidance when two rules conflict, as they often do. Most of our moral dilemmas, in fact, result from the clash of competing goods and values. Rule morality, then, must develop ways for us to arrange the rules in some kind of hierarchy, so that in cases of conflict, we can tell which rule to follow.

But once this process gets under way, we get into a bewildering maze of laws, priorities, exceptions, and qualifications; the clarity that made rule morality so attractive begins to disappear. This is what happened to the Jewish law, which was interpreted by generations of rabbis through the centuries to the point where the Talmud now constitutes a massive bank of legal precedents and opinions, through which the conscientious believer must thread.

Another hazard of rule morality is legalism, which exalts law over human needs. It is ironic that legalism has had such a vigorous history in the Christian community, when we consider how Jesus treated the legalism of his own day. His dictim, "The sabbath was made for man, not man for the sabbath," shows how far his own opposition to legalism had carried him. No wonder he offended the scribes and Pharisees (Mk. 2:27).

Finally, rule morality makes it easy for us to pass judgment upon other people. In our own case, we can usually find mitigating circumstances that make our violation of the rules seem justifiable. When I tell a lie, I may know that I did it for a good reason, so it was not really a moral offense. But I cannot see into the motives of another. All I can see is the lie, not the concerns that led the person into falsehood. It is easy for me to judge that other person to be at fault for breaking the rule about not telling a lie.

Antinomianism

"No Law"; "If it feels good, do it"

The complexity of rule morality and its tendency to exalt legalism above human needs has led, quite naturally, to a reaction against all laws. The traditional word for this position is "antinomianism," which means "against law."

Antinomianism has sometimes led to outrageous behavior. That is not surprising, since people who believe they can do just about anything they want are likely to do just that. In the early church, the antinomian view was upheld chiefly by Christians of gnostic background who believed that, since the spiritual world is the only important one, what you do with your body is morally indifferent.

Even though it has often led to lives of sheer pleasure-seeking, antinomianism does represent a legitimate ethical stance. It assumes that the person who is rightly disposed will always be led to do the right thing, with no need for rules or principles. One's intuition and sensitivity can be relied upon to guide the person to the right choice, just as radio signals lead the airline pilot to his proper destination—if he is tuned to the right wave length.

pre-ethical decision-making

The antinomian viewpoint is succinctly expressed in an aphorism attributed to St. Augustine, hardly an irresponsible pleasure seeker: "Love God and do as you please." As has been pointed out, that is not quite what Augustine said and certainly not what he meant.[2] But in its more colorful though less accurate form, the aphorism has been employed to justify the antinomian position. What it intends to say is that if you really love God, you will then want to do the just and loving thing: the good. So go ahead and do it.

The antinomian ethic has precisely the opposite advantages and disadvantages as the legalistic position. It is flexible and open to new situations. It travels light, without much philosophical baggage. It does not produce a proliferation of guidelines, as does rule morality. At its best it does express the heart of Christian ethics: "Love one another with brotherly affection" (Rom. 12:10).

But that very flexibility creates difficulties that make antinomianism less than practical for most of us. It puts entirely too much trust in feelings and attitudes. We all know of quite good-hearted people whose very good nature gets them into difficulties and causes trouble for others. It is not enough to have your heart in the right place; your head has to get into the ethical act too.

A well-disposed person, for example, may be moved to give charity to all who ask for it. Of course such a person will risk being victimized by unscrupulous people, but the person may know that and still not be deterred from giving. But almsgiving, however well intentioned, can create an unhealthy dependency in the recipient. The charitable person may actually be doing damage to those to whom the charity is done. In that case, the decision to pursue the unexamined good may be a wrong choice.

The antinomian who believes that "if it feels good, it is good," may be totally unaware of the damage that those good feelings can inflict on other people. This viewpoint has led to a considerable amount of sexual experimentation without any real personal commitment, the participants all the while blissfully unaware of the long-term personal destruction that may be taking place. It is easy to deceive ourselves about the effect of our actions in the lives of others, especially when we engage in those actions with the best of intentions.

Finally there is an element of sentimentality in the antinomian version of the love ethic in that it disregards our unconscious commitment to our own self-interest. Our responses are limited by the provinciality of our own perspective. The casual sexual experimentation can be justified on the ground that "nobody gets hurt." But without any consideration of principles, it is easy to avoid the question of what is really going on. When things go wrong in the relationship, who pays the price? One never knows what one may be doing to the other person if the ground rule is that we do not talk about principles, but only about feelings.

Situation Ethics

Situation ethics represents an attempt to get beyond both legalism and antinomianism by basing ethical judgments on the particular demands of the concrete situation. Although the term (and a companion term, "contextual ethics") have been used by students of Christian ethics for some time, situation ethics burst upon the public scene in 1966 with the publication of a controversial book by Joseph Fletcher, then a professor of Christian Ethics at Episcopal Theological School.[3] *Situation Ethics: The New Morality* was an immensely popular book which generated a number of responses, including at least two other books and hundreds of articles and reviews.[4]

The controversy was, to some extent, the result of matters which did not directly affect the central thesis of the book. It was written for popular consumption and therefore did not always include the careful qualifications that scholars in the field of ethics normally insist upon. Moreover the subtitle, *The New Morality,* made use of a phrase which was then in vogue to describe, not situation ethics, but rather the free-wheeling liberated sexual style of the mid-sixties. By making use of the term, Fletcher let himself in for a lot of unnecessary antagonism that had little to do with his main point.

But the notoriety of the book—and even the attacks upon it—helped to focus the debate about ethical norms and strategies. As a result, many Christians have learned about the method of situation ethics and how it can be used in making decisions about responsible Christian behavior.

Fletcher maintains that Christianity proposes only one ethical norm, principle, or rule—and that is love. His position might be summed up in the aphorism: "Love is not merely the best thing; it is the only thing." The right act in any situation is the loving thing. Moreover for Fletcher, the Christian ethic is not rule-centered, but person-centered. A loving act is one that helps people, not one that upholds an idea or concept.

This ethical view is both relativistic and pragmatic, as Fletcher concedes. It is relativist because there is only one absolute: love. All other values are relative to that one absolute. It is pragmatic because it judges the quality of acts by their consequences. There is no intrinsic value in any particular act. Each act takes its value from the effects it produces.

In the situation described by Kant, Fletcher would have no trouble in approving the lie told by the person facing the potential murderer. The lie would be a loving act because it would save the life of the victim and would save the would-be murderer from committing a serious crime. On the whole, Fletcher would agree, it is right to tell the truth. But in any particular situation, that general rule has to be tested against the absolute demand to do the loving thing.

Fletcher is less persuasive when he argues that, once the loving action is discerned, one can perform the action in the assurance that it will be unambiguously right. He refuses to concede the possibility that a loving action may nevertheless produce evil as well as good. He has no patience with the view that in some situations the best we can do is the "lesser evil."[5]

John C. Bennett criticizes this view because it would ignore the tension that is an inevitable part of the moral life.[6] In making a moral choice, I may find myself in a situation in which there are genuine goods and evils in several possible courses of action. Suppose I take the course which I believe to be the most loving. Should I then simply refuse to think any longer about the values that I decided against? If I do, I may feel more confident about my decision, but I will have lost any sense of the relativity of that choice, or of the evil that I might have done while doing the good.

It may be right and just—and even loving, as Fletcher understands the word—for me to kill an enemy in wartime. But in so doing, I cannot afford the luxury of believing that my action has no evil in it. The death of a fellow human can never be other than evil, no matter how necessary it might have been. If we lose sight of the evil involved in our own right choices, we will develop a callous attitude that will make love more restrictive rather than more universal in its application.

Finally, Fletcher's understanding of situation ethics has been faulted for its lack of capacity to deal with issues in the larger arena of society and politics. Fletcher's illustrations are mostly of interpersonal relationships; he has little to say about how a society makes decisions about economic issues, labor disputes, war and peace, social policy.[7]

While that criticism is valid as far as Fletcher's book is concerned, it would be a mistake to see situation ethics as applying only to interpersonal behavior. On the contrary, as we begin to examine more complex social and political issues, it will become clear that Niebuhr's question—"What is going on?"—is more and more significant. Our responses to social issues will be determined largely by our reading of the facts of each case. It will become obvious that no two situations are exactly alike. In discussing these issues, we make use of the situation ethics approach whether we are aware of it or not.

CASUISTRY

"Rules have underlying *Principles*."

One indirect result of Fletcher's attack upon legalism has been a renewed effort to restate what is meant by ethical norms and principles. Not all principled thinking is legalistic. Much of it is motivated by the same concern for love that Fletcher finds central to the Christian life.

But the situationist approach, many would claim, tends to overemphasize the uniqueness of each particular ethical decision. In real life, it is only on relatively rare occasions that we find ourselves in situations that can be called unique. The same issues come up again and again in the lives of different people. When we find ourselves confronted by a moral dilemma, we can be sure that other faithful Christians have faced similar situations; we can learn something from their experience.

That experience is reflected in those rules that presume to tell us what we ought to do and not do in particular situations. The commandment "Thou shalt not steal" describes what is permissible or not permissible in a wide variety of situations. When I see a blanket hanging on someone's clothesline, I do not have to engage in deep reflection to know that I ought not take it for my own. I do not have to wonder whether or not it is all right to walk out of a store with a piece of merchandise I have not paid for. My obligations in those instances are quite adequately described by the rules. Loving action is spelled out for me in advance.

But are there not situations where the rule has to be suspended in the name of love? How about the case of a man who steals a loaf of bread from a rich man's kitchen in order to feed his starving children? Would that not be a case of violating a rule in the name of love?

Many traditional ethical thinkers would argue that this case requires us to clarify what we mean by stealing. If stealing is taking from another what belongs to that other, against the reasonable will of that other, then what we are considering is not stealing at all, but an act of simple justice. Only a legalistic understanding of the word "steal," one that absolutizes the right of private property, would call the poor man's act stealing.

This mode of ethical reflection has been called "casuistry," the process of applying principles to actual cases. The word has a bad connotation for many of us, but that is a matter of history. The Jesuit Order developed the art of casuistry to a high degree some centuries ago. It was commonly said that, if you granted a Jesuit his premise, he could argue you into anything. Fortunately Jesuits no longer do that sort of thing and their good name has been rehabilitated. Perhaps it is time to rehabilitate the word *casuistry* as well.

To apply a principle to a case, you have to know the principle. What does it require? What does it mean? What value does it support? Then you have to know the case. What is going on? What is the meaning and significance of the acts we are considering? Only then can we ask: How does the principle fit the case? Only then can we make the judgment of what response is indicated. Fletcher would probably call this process legalistic. I would suggest that it becomes legalistic only when we look at the law literalistically, when we consider only the letter and not the spirit of the law.

The distinction between rules and principles is not a very clear one. Generally, rules prescribe specific actions: "Always tell the truth." Principles describe more general kinds of conduct: "Our dealings with other people should be characterized by honesty and integrity." The *rule* about truthtelling serves the *principle* of honesty and integrity in interpersonal relations. It describes how we ought to relate to other people. Our speech opens to another what is inside us: our feelings and perceptions, as well as our ideas. Love demands truthfulness in the name of authentic interpersonal relationships. If I do not tell the truth, I do not reveal my real self to the other person.

But how about the example that Kant discusses: the man bent on murder who demands to know where his victim is hiding? As in the case of the rule about stealing, this situation calls for a more precise statement of what we mean by lying and truth-telling. Let us define the truth-telling rule as:

α   "It is wrong to tell a lie to someone who has a right to the truth." That definition would permit the excusable lie in cases where telling the truth would not serve the purposes of either love or personal integrity.

For example: a single woman meets a man at a party. After being in his company for a short time, she finds him rather strange and even a little frightening. He asks where she lives and for her telephone number. The right-to-the-truth rule would make it legitimate for her to give him a false name or a false address in order to protect her privacy.

This restatement of the rule solves the problem of the diplomatic lie. "How did you like the play?" he asks on their first date. Actually, it was a bomb, but does he really need to know that? Wouldn't a modest, "It was fine," be better than the unvarnished truth? When a friend asks, "How are you?" does he really need to know that in fact you're feeling terrible this morning? A genteel suppression of the whole truth might be the best social lubricant in some situations. "You should always tell the truth to someone who has a right to it." That seems to be a reasonably adequate statement of the rule.

But the rule is important insofar as it serves the underlying ethical principle, in this case the principle of honesty and integrity in interpersonal relationships. Every lapse from truth-telling weakens the principle, so that even if the rule does not seem to apply, it should be seriously considered before opting for the right-to-know escape clause.

When stated clearly and thoughtfully, rules can serve principles. And principles can serve the purposes of love by offering summary guidance for what love will require in situations that tend to recur. Those who emphasize the use of principles stress the continuity of ethical situations; that is what makes rules and principles useful. Those who emphasize the situation tend to focus on the exceptional case in an effort to discredit the universal applicability of rules.

Fletcher For the most part, our moral choices do follow the rules with no great difficulty. Our dilemmas occur when rules and principles collide, where values conflict and compete. The deciding person is called to exercise judgment as to which

See "Norms," Westminster Ethics, p. 26; an absolute norm.

rules or principles will carry the greatest weight in that particular situation.

Natural Law

Our discussion has assumed that rules and principles constitute the accumulated wisdom of past experience of bringing love to bear on moral choices. But are there also general, universal principles that apply to all people everywhere? Is there something that could be described as an ethic of natural law?

This question has been discussed for centuries, by philosophers and theologians, both within and outside the Christian church. The philosophical question is: "Is there in humankind some universal ethical sense which can be appealed to in the final analysis?" In theological terms the question becomes: "Has God made his intentions known to all people so that, by use of their reasoning powers, they can perceive and know the good?"

Paul believed so:

> . . . what can be known about God is plain to them, because God has shown it to them. Ever since the creation of the world, his invisible nature, namely, his eternal power and deity, has been clearly perceived in the things that have been made. So they are without excuse (Rom. 1:19–20).

Traditional Roman Catholic moral theology has been based on the assumption that there is a moral law of nature which all people are bound to obey and that it is discoverable by human reason. Protestant thinkers have been less impressed by the claims of natural law ethics, partly because of the difficulties it has created for Roman Catholics.

One problem is that the Roman Catholic version of natural law develops out of Aristotelian philosophy, as interpreted by Thomas Aquinas. This tradition tends to absolutize ethical positions in a static manner that most non-Roman Catholics do not find persuasive. The best contemporary example of this problem is the recent papal encyclical, *Humanae*

Vitae, which forbids the use of artificial methods of contraception for birth control and family planning.

The natural law view is that sexual intercourse is intended for the procreation of children. Any interference with that process by artificial means is, therefore, sinful because it frustrates the intention of God as revealed in that natural process. A society that lives by interfering with natural processes (by interposing other natural processes) will hardly find such reasoning conclusive, especially in view of the worldwide population explosion which seems to demand responsible efforts to control the size of families.

This process of reaching moral conclusions by syllogistic reasoning from premises rests on shaky ground. Many contemporary Roman Catholic moral theologians are moving away from this kind of thinking without giving up the idea of natural law. They assert that there is, indeed, a "law of our being as humans," obedience to which fulfills our deepest human purposes and thereby constitutes the good. They recognize that our perception of this natural law will differ according to time and place, which means that we can enter more deeply into an understanding of what the natural law is and what it requires of us.[8]

We could point, for example, to how our understanding of our obligation to others has widened with the passing centuries. Most people today would conceive of humanity as a single unit. All people are brothers and sisters under God. In more primitive societies, humanity was bounded by the tribe itself. There was one law for "people" and another law for outsiders: the stranger, the gentile, the barbarian. Today a natural law ethic would recognize no such distinctions.

As our perceptions of natural law have changed, Protestant thinkers have begun to discover its usefulness. John C. Bennett, for example, sees natural law as offering the possibility that Christian ethical reflection can find common ground with non-Christians as both appeal to an ethic that can be validated by human reason without appeal to a special revelation.[9]

The biblical revelation and the historical experience of the church provide the Christian with resources for ethical reflection that are not available to the non-Christian. But if the results of that reflection are valid, they should commend themselves to all seekers of the good and ought to be capable of validation through the use of human reason.

This is a very promising direction for ethical thought to be taking in our pluralistic era. It is part of the drive toward a universal ethic (a method, perhaps, rather than a system; some common values and assumptions, rather than a code) that can be accepted by all people, that is applicable to all people, and that is open to change as the state of our knowledge changes.

Moral Presumptions

As a way of bringing principles to bear on concrete situations, Philip Wogaman makes use of the idea of moral presumptions. When a moral choice is to be made, the Christian comes into the situation already equipped with the demand to do the loving thing; on that nearly all ethical thinkers would agree. But love predisposes the Christian to a certain preliminary bias in some very specific directions. That is to say, as Christians we are prejudiced in favor of some things and against other things.[10]

War, for example, poses an ethical dilemma for the Christian. The Christian harbors a deep-seated prejudice against war because violence and killing are contrary to what love demands. Some Christians take the view that this prejudice makes participation in any war impossible; they can be called pacifists. Most other Christians do not take the pacifist view because they recognize that in some situations it might be more ethically responsible—indeed, more loving—to fight a war on behalf of justice than to refuse to fight.

Nevertheless a decision for war can never be made easily. So in any situation where the question of war comes up, the Christian will begin with the view that, on the whole, war is to be avoided. This is what Wogaman calls a presumption in favor of peace and against war.

The decision for going to war, therefore, must bear the burden of proof. Unless the case for war can be proved beyond a reasonable doubt, then the Christian will decide against it. This process works very much like the presumption in our legal system that favors the accused, who is presumed to be innocent until proven guilty beyond a reasonable doubt. The accused does not have to prove innocence; the prosecution has to prove guilt. It is the same with the war/peace issue. Peace needs no justification; it is the normative (right) state of affairs. The decision for war does need justification because the Christian moral presumption is against it.

As we have already seen, there may be cases where the taking of someone else's property is justifiable. But the Christian moral presumption is against the taking of the property of another. The burden of proof, therefore, rests on the person who would take the property.

Are there any presumptions that all Christians would share? Wogaman thinks so. He identifies four positive presumptions and two negative ones. On the positive side, most Christians would affirm the goodness of the created order, the value of human life, the unity of the human family in God, and the equality of persons in God. Negatively he mentions human finitude, which limits our perception of the good; and human sinfulness, which predisposes us to act in our own interest.[11] Our ethical reflection has to recognize our tendency to favor our own cause in making our decisions.

The usefulness of Wogaman's work is that it helps us to identify the "tilt" in Christian thinking about ethical issues. It suggests how we can bring rules and principles into our reflection without absolutizing them, how we can make use of "moral laws" without lapsing into legalism. Rules and principles enter into our reflection as presumptions which affirm our commitments and place the burden of proof on the decision to act contrary to them.

This concept helps us to see that, as Christians, we do not make moral choices in a vacuum. We stand in a tradition, in a community of faith and moral commitment. While we may have to make our moral choices alone, nevertheless we are not without resources for guidance and direction. We are surrounded by a great cloud of witnesses.

Base Points for Ethical Reflection

Before leaving this discussion of ethical decision-making, perhaps we can put it into a larger perspective. The debate of "situation versus principle" has been going on in professional circles for more than a decade. It is sometimes hard for the lay person to follow because ethical thinkers, like most scholars, are not always at their best in such debates. They tend to oversimplify, caricature, and even distort the viewpoints of their adversaries.

Thus Joseph Fletcher has characterized any ethical perspective not focused on the situation as "legalism." His opponents have castigated his views as soulless, permissive, even sub-Christian. Frederick D. Maurice long ago taught us that we are likely to be right in what we affirm and wrong in what we deny. This observation is certainly borne out in the debate over "situation versus principle" in Christian ethics.

One of our most astute ethical thinkers, James Gustafson, moved the discussion beyond the level of debate well before the debate got underway in earnest. For Gustafson, the debate was misplaced because: "It has tended to assume that the matter of how moral decisions are made could be separated from other considerations."[12]

In point of fact, Gustafson notes, ethical thinkers may begin with a consideration of the actual moral situation or the moral context or, alternatively, may begin with fixed principles. But most responsible moralists actually move through a consideration of four "base points" in their process of ethical reflection. These points are: (1) the situation in which the decision is to be made, (2) the principles on which it is to be made, (3) the theological rationale for those principles, and (4) the nature of the Christian life in Christ.[13] This last consideration refers us back to our previous discussion of the moral agent, the person who has to make the decision.

While ethical thinkers may be identified by their starting

point—one is called a situationist, another a principled thinker, etc.—in arriving at judgments they tend to touch all four of those bases. To argue for one point over against another, therefore, is a mistake which merely leads to polarization of the matter under discussion.

Fletcher himself alludes to Gustafson's essay (which was originally published the year before his own book) in a rather approving way. He seems to repudiate the debate himself when he says,

> There is no real quarrel here between situationism and an ethic of principles, unless the principles are hardened into laws.[14]

I mention this because I think that Gustafson has hit upon what most Christians, aside from professional students of ethics, would find to be their own method for ethical reflection. By and large we begin with the situation because something has happened that requires a response from us. But we have already committed ourselves to some principles. We already make certain presumptions, which we carry into our consideration of the situation. We may not have thought through the theological rationale for our views, but most of us have an operational theology of sorts, whether we can articulate it or not. Finally we enter such situations as moral agents whose character has been formed by our previous experience, which includes our apprenticeship in the body of Christ.

Thus our ethical decisions may incorporate all of these base points. We may not be equally conscious of all of them at any one time, but knowing that they are in the background can encourage us to bring to the surface those components of our decision-making that we have not thought about previously. Only thus can we be sure that we have given full credit to all aspects of our moral life.

Or are "they" immune to this process?

· 4 ·

Biblical Resources
for Ethical Reflection

Christians naturally turn to the Bible for moral guidance, for the Bible is our fundamental authority in religious matters. Yet in using the Bible, we need to exercise care and discrimination in order to avoid distorting its message. For the Bible is not a single book, but a collection of books, an incredibly diverse assortment of literary forms: stories, history, visions, proverbs, etc. It was not written primarily to tell contemporary men and women how to behave. It was written to bear witness to God's saving acts, to remind us of what God has done in history, for us and for our salvation.

History and Biblical Interpretation

We read the Bible through the filter of thousands of years of history. These documents were written in eras very different from our own, against a background of cultural assumptions that we can only dimly perceive. When the ancient writers render judgments about the events they describe, we can sometimes share their interpretations. At other times, however, we simply cannot see what they are trying to say.

Our incomprehension should come as no surprise, for in our own time we have learned that it takes years of living in another culture to even begin to understand it. If that is true in the case of other contemporary cultures, how much more difficult will it be to understand civilizations that have been gone for more than two thousand years. Scholars have tried to unravel the mysteries of these ancient societies, but have only begun to scratch the surface.

Because of this long gap in time, our approach to Scripture brings us up against the issue of timeless truths versus time-conditioned values. As we read the biblical literature, how much of it is truth that still holds good for us and what has to be dismissed as pertinent only to the age in which it was written?

The question brings us close to the heart of biblical faith, which is based on the conviction that God, the Lord of history, reveals himself in the particularity of time and place. He is not the abstract "first cause" of the philosophers, but the loving, judging God of Israel. His only once-for-all revelation is not a piece of information, but a person: Jesus Christ, against whom every truth, every value, every law or principle is to be measured.

This recognition of the time-conditioned character of the biblical literature is no new insight. In the passage referred to earlier, Richard Hooker draws attention to Leviticus 19 which includes the command: "You shall love your neighbor as yourself" (18). In the following verse, we read: "You shall not sow your field with two kinds of seed; nor shall there come upon you a garment made of two kinds of stuff" (19).

Hooker concedes that he does not know why the Lord saw fit to give Israel this commandment. He suggests that, since our reason does not disclose to us any cause for it, we are not bound to observe it. Thus Hooker would say that while the command to love our neighbor is binding upon us, this other command is not.[1]

Jesus' own teachings share this time-conditioned character. A century ago, Jesus was regarded by many as a great moral teacher who introduced to the world a higher set of ideals than had ever been known before. That view of Jesus, however, has been pretty much exploded by more recent New Testament study. The result of that exploration is the recognition that Jesus did not see himself—nor did his contemporaries see him—as primarily a teacher of ethics.

reason over law.

THE COMING KINGDOM

The center of Jesus' ministry was the proclamation of a new era: the messianic age. His essential message was, "Repent, for the kingdom of heaven is at hand" (Mt. 4:17). He saw himself as the bearer of that kingdom; he called people to take their stand for him and for the good news that he proclaimed. Jesus' message was first of all religious: it had to do with what God was doing in the world. Only as a consequence of that proclamation was he a teacher of ethics.

Jesus' teaching was shaped by his expectation that the present age was coming to a rapid end. Thus when he announced, "I have come to set a man against his father, and a daughter against her mother" (Mt. 10:35), he was not condemning family life; he was speaking of the kingdom. When the call to the kingdom comes, it takes the highest priority. Nothing can stand in its way, not even the most important relationships of ordinary life. When we read that passage today, we have to understand it in the context of Jesus' anticipation of the coming kingdom. (which doesn't change the truth of this statement one iota!)

Biblical Faith and Ethics

Contemporary biblical scholars have pointed out that, properly speaking, the Bible knows nothing of ethics. There is no discussion in the biblical literature of ethical principles, the good life, or any of the kind of moral issues that so captivated the minds of Greek thinkers like Plato, Aristotle, and Epicurus.

In the Old Testament, human behavior is prescribed by the law of the Lord. The binding force of the law is the covenant. The binding force of the covenant is the Exodus. The primary fact of Israel's life is that God rescued Israel from Egypt. God led Israel through the wilderness and promised them the land of Canaan. To seal his promise, God made a covenant with Israel: "Now therefore, if you will obey my voice and keep my covenant, you shall be my own possession among all the peoples"(Ex. 19:5).

Then, so that the children of Israel would know what was

but see O.T. Ethics, concerning this paper and their understanding of where proselytes behavior come from expected of them, God gave the law to Moses. Israel was bound to keep the law as its part of the covenant. But the law was not perceived as a burden to be tolerated; it was valued and honored as the gift of a loving God. Psalm 119, a lengthy devotional meditation on the law, contains phrases such as this: "Behold, my delight is in thy commandments" (40). Even today, Jews recite a prayer that concludes, "Blessed art Thou, O Lord God, giver of the law." The life of the Jew, then, is a grateful and loving response to the good God who has already acted to redeem Israel. *AMEN*

In the New Testament, the moral life occupies a similar place, for the center of the New Testament is the proclamation of the Gospel: Jesus the risen Lord has saved us from sin and death. By his death and resurrection, he has made God's love and forgiveness available to all people. Through repentance and baptism, the Christian is brought into the kingdom of grace and enabled to live a new life in the power of the Holy Spirit. This new life is lived out in the spirit-filled community of faith, the church, which is the body of Christ.

The Christian life is a response of love and gratitude to the loving God who has brought salvation in Jesus Christ. Ethical teaching is important as an aid to understanding what the new life in Christ looks like here and now. Thus the moral life becomes the fruit of the Spirit, not the means of grace.

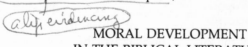

MORAL DEVELOPMENT
IN THE BIBLICAL LITERATURE

The extraordinary diversity of biblical material makes it difficult to identify any single ethical tradition in the Bible. It is misleading, therefore, to take any single verse from Scripture and use it to make a moral judgment on a contemporary situation. Each passage has to be seen in its own context and in the wider context of the entire Bible.

The theory of moral development referred to in chapter 2 may help us to sort out some of this diverse material. As ethical issues arise in people's lives, their own state of moral development will color their perception of those events which have moral significance for them. From this perspective, we can discern in the Bible evidence of punishment orientation, law-and-order orientation, and an orientation toward universal ethical principles, to take only the most obvious categories.

Kohlberg
maleg,
pp. 26 ff

Punishment/Obedience Orientation

The essence of this orientation is that if you do something wrong, something terrible is going to happen to you. Examples of this view of life abound in the Old Testament: the story of the flood (Gen. 6–9); the fate of Sodom and Gomorrah (Gen. 18–19); Korah's rebellion against Moses (Num. 16); and the story of Elisha and the she-bears (2 Kg. 2:23–25).

This orientation was embedded in the consciousness of Israel, finally developing into a providential theory of history. Defeat in war, misfortune, even natural disasters were seen as punishment for evil deeds. The prophetic writings are full of dire predictions of what the Lord will do to his faithless people if they do not repent. (E.g., Is. 9:8–21; Jer. 16:1–13; Am. 3:12–4:12.)

Torah and prophets, psalms and proverbs all testify to the belief that Israel's sinfulness leads to misfortune, suffering, and defeat. Yet while our evil deeds often do lead to disaster, the good do not always prevail, nor do the wicked always suffer. The book of Job represents one attempt to move beyond the punishment/obedience orientation by looking honestly at the suffering of the innocent.

When Job is struck by the loss of his family, his property, and his health, when he is left scratching his boils on the ash heap, his friends come by to comfort him. They trot out the stock answer to his dilemma: he must have sinned, whether he knows it or not, or else he would not have suffered such calamities. But Job will have none of it. He demands to know by what right he is being punished. Then the Lord appears to him and demands to know by what right Job even asks the question. But the Lord goes on to commend Job because, though uncomprehending, Job has remained faithful. But still the Lord does not give Job any reason for his unmerited suffering. Thus, while the book of Job does not answer the question of why the innocent suffer, it does subvert the traditional connection between disobedience and divine punishment.

In the New Testament, Jesus carries this repudiation one step further. He calls on his followers to love even their enemies so that they can be like their Father in heaven, "for he makes his sun rise on the evil and on the good, and sends rain on the just and on the unjust" (Mt. 5:45). In other words, for Jesus, the motive for doing good is not to avoid punishment by an angry God but to imitate the loving God who cares even for those who hate him.

Law-and-Order Orientation

As noted earlier, ancient Israel had no "ethic." What it had was the law of the Lord. That law includes moral precepts, of course, but it also included ceremonial rules, food regulations, and curious provisions like the one about not sowing two kinds of seed. All of these injunctions were of equal value to the Israelite, for they were all part of the law, God's requirement for maintaining the covenant.

The prophets of Israel focus their complaints against the people on their failure to keep the law. Thus in Amos, Judah is judged, "because they have rejected the law of the Lord and have not kept his statutes" (2:4). Jeremiah appeals to the covenant and accuses the people of disobedience (11:1–8). Hosea compares the faithlessness of Israel to the faithlessness of a harlot wife (1:2). In the Psalms and the Wisdom literature, the righteous person is the one who keeps the law.

The defect of the law-and-order mentality is its tendency toward legalism and moralism. The first would concentrate on the letter of the law rather than its spirit; the second would make use of the law to condemn other people. Neither of these tendencies appear in the Old Testament to any significant extent, but they are evident in the tradition of the Pharisees in Jesus' time. Jesus opposes these tendencies, even to the extent of qualifying, altering, and in some cases intensifying the demands of the law.

Thus the command to do no murder is expanded: "But I say to you, that everyone who is angry with his brother shall be liable to judgment" (Mt. 5:22). Adultery is extended to apply to anyone who looks at a woman lustfully. The demand to love one's neighbor is extended to a demand to love one's enemies as well. Thus, while Jesus did not repudiate the law, he moved beyond the law-and-order orientation to the level of the universal principles that underlie the law.

Universal Ethical Principle Orientation

It would be a mistake to contrast the law-and-order orientation of the Old Testament with the "ethical principle" orientation of the New, for there is considerable evidence of a movement toward universal principles in the Old Testament itself.

The prophetic literature includes a number of proclamations of universal principle. Among the most often cited are those from Amos:

I hate, I despise your feasts,
And I take no delight in your solemn assemblies. . . .
But let justice roll down like waters,
And righteousness like an ever-flowing stream (5:21, 24).

And from Micah:

He has showed you, O man, what is good;
And what does the Lord require of you
But to do justice, and to love kindness,
And to walk humbly with your God? (6:8).

Finally, Jeremiah points the way toward the new covenant as the Lord proclaims: "I will put my law within them and I will write it on their hearts" (31:33). When the spirit of the law is in the heart, internalized we would say, there is no longer any need to rely on prescriptions and commandments.

That promise comes to fruition in Jesus' teaching of the centrality of love: absolute, unqualified, unlimited. Love for God and love for the neighbor, who is anyone in need. Love leads Jesus to heal on the sabbath because the sabbath was made for man, not man for the sabbath. Love abolishes the food laws because, "Not what goes into the mouth defiles a man, but what comes out of the mouth" (Mt. 15:11). Love dictates that those who feed the hungry and clothe the naked will enter into the kingdom because they have ministered to the king himself, even though they did not know it.

The commitment to love as the center of the moral life is carried on in the teaching of the early church, as evidenced by the epistles of John and Paul. Paul's diatribes against the law have to be seen as part of his protest against the legalism of the pharisaical tradition. He regards the law as "Our custodian until Christ came" (Gal. 3:24), but it is now transcended by the covenant of grace.

Still Paul does not neglect the law's demands but rather puts them into the context of the command to love. "Love does no wrong to a neighbor," he writes. "Therefore love is the fulfilling of the law" (Rom. 13:9–10). John says very much the same thing: "Beloved, let us love one another; for love is of God, and he who loves is born of God and knows God. He who does not love does not know God; for God is love" (1 Jn 4:7–8).

Thus the law-and-order orientation is left behind in favor of a commitment to love, which represents for the Christian, not just God's commandment but God's very being. To love is to please God; more than that, to love is to be like God.

This discussion of moral development is not based on the outmoded concept of "progressive revelation." That idea, popular in the early part of this century, described the ancient Hebrews as an unenlightened and barbarous people who nevertheless developed very high religious concepts: the idea of one God, the idea of moral excellence, the idea of love, etc., until they produced the finest flower of the moral life: Jesus of Nazareth. The implication of this view was that mankind has continued its onward and upward path right up until our own time, which represents the climax of humanity's moral striving.

The course of recent history has laid that idea to rest. Biblical scholarship has also demonstrated that the idea of progress fits most uncomfortably into the framework of biblical thought. Nevertheless, as our illustrations suggest, there is evidence of moral development in the Bible, though various stages can be seen to coexist at the same historical moment.

There is no reason for us to claim superiority for one stage over another. Much less can we assert our own superiority over those men and women of biblical times who sought to live out their faithfulness in the context of their own history. Still I would expect that people who read the Bible today will resonate to those stories and precepts that correspond most closely with their own stage of moral development. And since we are called to exercise our own reasoning powers in the study of Scripture, it is surely valid for us to make judgments as to which materials we find most helpful in our own moral pilgrimage.

Moral Presumptions of the Biblical Literature

It is possible to select from the mass of biblical material a number of moral presumptions shared by many of the writers. These would include the presumptions already identified by Wogaman (see chapter 3), the moral model of "the righ- *(p.44)* teous" (see chapter 2), and the central biblical values of love and justice. Let us single out, in addition, two other presumptions, one positive and one negative.

FAVORING THE POOR

The Bible is clearly prejudiced in favor of the most vulnerable members of the community: the fatherless, the widow, the sojourner, and especially the poor. These groups need special protection because they have no powerful defender to come to their aid. The fatherless and widows have no man to protect them. The sojourner, being an outsider, is likely to be treated with suspicion and hostility. The poor are exploited or forgotten. Both Isaiah and Ezekiel advocate feeding the hungry and clothing the naked (Is. 58:7; Ezek. 18:16). Amos denounces the greedy,

> Because they sell the righteous for silver
> and the needy for a pair of shoes—
> they that trample the head of the poor
> into the dust of the earth (2:6–7).

(3) probably Niebuhr's "Man the answerer", p.25.

Jesus likewise singles out the poor as blessed, for the kingdom of heaven is theirs (Lk. 6:20). The righteous gain entrance into the kingdom on the basis of their treatment of the hungry, the naked, the stranger, the sick (Mt. 25:31–46). In the light of this presumption, therefore, Jesus' observation that "The poor you always have with you" (Jn. 12:8) is not to be seen as a callous indifference to their plight but as a sober recognition that because of human sinfulness we can expect that there will always be poor in the land.

Concern for the poor is somewhat muted in the epistles, but both Paul and James speak of the need to remember the poor and to give alms (2 Cor. 9:9; Jas. 2:2–6). The infrequency of these references may be due to the fact that most of the early Christians were poor themselves. They were surely not in any position to exploit anyone.

AGAINST IDOLATRY

Idolatry can consist of making an image and worshiping it, bowing down at the high places, eating on the mountain, offering sons and daughters for sacrifice; as well as divination, soothsaying, and sorcery. "High places" and "mountains" are significant because that is where the shrines of the gods of the land were located.

These practices are condemned, not merely in the interest of the purity of religion. The prophets knew that following false gods constituted a betrayal of the covenant. The pagan gods were amoral; they had no interest in the ethical character of human behavior. Thus when people abandoned the Lord of Israel in favor of these false gods, they were also likely to commit injustices and to behave licentiously. The fact that idolatry and injustice are frequently mentioned together shows how close these two evils were associated in the minds of the prophets. (See, e.g., Hab. 2:12–19.)

These presumptions show something of the direction of ethical thought in the biblical literature. They indicate that God's concern for justice is not a mere balancing of opposing forces, but that it includes a particular kind of care for those most in need of care. God's demand for loyalty is not mere supernatural jealousy but a passion for the fulfillment of the covenant on the part of the covenant people.

Using the Bible for Ethical Reflection

From what has been said so far, it seems clear that using the Bible in our ethical reflection may not be such a simple process as we have been led to believe. While the Bible comprises a variety of material, all of which is relevant, none of that material may bear directly on the matter at hand. The Bible was not intended to be a source book for moral teaching. The writers, for the most part, had other intentions and purposes. We do violence to the material when we try to wring from it clear and specific answers to our own ethical questions.

How then are we to use the Bible? We can answer that more clearly, perhaps, after we have considered and rejected some wrong ways of using biblical materials.

THE MORALIZING FALLACY

Our first temptation is to moralize every story, whether appropriate or not. Many of us have had to endure the moralizing efforts of Sunday School teachers who have ruined forever for us such powerful but ambiguous tales as the story of Jacob and Esau. When Jacob cheats Esau of his birthright, when he goes into his father Isaac disguised as Esau so as to procure his father's blessing, he is not offering a moral example for the young. Jacob is a rascal, a genial and engaging rascal to be sure, but nevertheless a liar and a cheat. If we are true to the material, we can hardly present him as anything else.

THE LITERALIST FALLACY

A second temptation is to absolutize every provision and to try to apply its literal meaning. The commandment to make no graven image, for example, has traditionally been taken quite literally be Jews. As a result, they do not represent the human figure in the synagogue. Moslems, likewise interpreting the prohibition literally, have developed a highly stylized form of nonrepresentational art which carefully avoids any depiction of the creature. Because St. Paul observed that women should keep silence in the churches, many Christians believe that women should not be ordained to the Christian ministry.

THE RATIONALIST FALLACY

A third temptation is to bring to our consideration of the biblical text the presuppositions and value assumptions of our own cultural heritage, picking and choosing from the biblical literature whatever best fits our preconceptions. Thus Thomas Jefferson edited the New Testament, omitting any reference to miracle or other elements uncongenial to his rationalistic temperament.

FROM TEXT TO CONTEXT

If we are to avoid those temptations, how are we to deal with biblical material, preserving both the integrity of the text and our own integrity as reasoning moral agents?

Once we have read a biblical passage thoroughly, we should study it in its context in order to understand the meaning and significance of the act, story, or commandment. What, for example, is the meaning of the prohibition of graven images? The central issue, of course, is not art but idolatry—the worship of the creature instead of the creator. If that is the case, it is beside the point to eliminate sculpture and painting from worship and life. Indeed, the visual arts can be an aid to worship and meditation, by opening us up to the divine creativity. We can dare to use graven images, then, if we can do so without taking them too seriously, without according them the place that belongs to God alone. Then we will have fulfilled the intention of the commandment.

SCRIPTURE INTERPRETS SCRIPTURE

Despite the variety of biblical materials, there are some central themes that run through the entire literature. It is important, then, that we learn to see each passage in the light of the whole Bible. Each particular verse, story, or rule, has to be viewed in a total perspective, in the context of what God is doing and what his activity means for us. Thus Jacob may be no moral hero, but he is one of the patriarchs. When we see his place in the divine plan of salvation history, we may be led to understand how God can use the most unpromising human material to further his purposes.

THE BIBLE AND MORAL DEVELOPMENT

Finally, it should be stressed that the most important function of the Bible in the Christian life is not its treatment of particular issues, but its contribution to the formation of moral character. Christians who read and study the Bible on some regular basis, who immerse themselves in the text, who take it seriously and listen to what it has to say to them, such people will, over the long haul, be formed and shaped by that experience. They will begin to look at the world from the standpoint of biblical faith, a stance which will put them in tension with the values and presuppositions of their culture. They will bring to their ethical reflection the moral presumptions of biblical faith, without being overly self-conscious about the matter.

Used in this way, the Bible can speak to our generation just as it has spoken to generations of Christians in the past. It will bring to our moral dilemmas an influence that bears authority without inhibiting the use of human reason, and without undermining that freedom which is the most precious heritage of the Gospel of Christ.[2]

② as the H.S. brings to life the scriptures in particular situations, the rhema of God.

Part Two

―――

MORAL ISSUES
IN PERSONAL LIVING

―――

· 5 ·

Running Your Own Life

"Love your neighbor as yourself." That is the norm for Christian living. It implies that love of self is natural and legitimate. But how am I to go about loving myself? Are there ethical issues in the running of my own life? Or is what I do by myself, to myself, strictly my own business as long as I do not step on anyone else's toes?

This question takes on a special significance in our individualistic age. In our society, people are burdened with a heightened sense of self that, while legitimate at its best, tends to limit our vision and cut us off from the world outside the self.

The Temple of the Holy Spirit

The Bible knows no such individualistic perspective, for it sees human life lived out under the searching gaze of the Almighty. No human act is without significance. Everything we are or do, think or feel, is subject to divine judgment. Paul expresses the biblical view most succinctly:

> Do you not know that your body is a temple of the Holy Spirit within you, which you have from God? You are not your own; you were bought with a price. So glorify God in your body (1 Cor. 6:19–20).

Our lives are a gift which we receive in trust. We are accountable to God for our stewardship of that gift, just as in the biblical parable the servants who received talents from their master were held responsible for their use of those talents (Mt. 25:14–30).

Decisions about what we will do with our lives are inevitably shaped by our religious convictions. If you believe that you owe your life to God and are responsible to him for the use you make of it, you will make one kind of choice. You will make quite different choices if you see your life as a mere biological accident, without meaning or purpose.

ME-ISM

Journalist Tom Wolfe has called this the "Me Decade."[1] He was referring, of course, to the widespread preoccupation with the self that seems characteristic of our society. It is typified by such popular book titles as *How to Be Your Own Best Friend, Winning through Intimidation,* and *Looking out for Number One.* The proliferation of modish self-help therapies is another indication of what Wolfe is describing.

Self-preoccupation in itself is nothing new. We humans have always shown a tendency to look out for ourselves. But throughout the Christian era we have been taught that selfishness and self-centeredness are manifestations of human sinfulness. In the past our religious convictions have led us to be ashamed of our selfishness and to confess it as sin.

Today, however, we are witnessing a militant repudiation of altruism and concern for others. Our society has made a virtue of this self-preoccupation.

To be sure, the Gospel does not condemn self-love. The commandment, after all, is to love your neighbor as yourself, not instead of yourself. Paul is even more explicit about self-affirmation when he points out, "No man ever hates his own flesh, but nourishes and cherishes it" (Eph. 5:29). This fact deserves to be emphasized, because some Christian teaching has tended to downgrade the self. Love of neighbor has sometimes been interpreted to mean that it is sinful to look after our own interests. Humility has often been understood to mean that we should regard ourselves as no-account worms.

The Christian understanding of the self begins with the affirmation of the self. We are right to assert our own dignity and worth. We are made in God's image; Christ died for us. God loves us. We are important; we count.

If you really believe that, then you have no need to be constantly taking your psychological pulse, wondering, "How am I doing?" "What do they really think of me?" If you can honestly and genuinely affirm yourself, then you can stop worrying about yourself and get on to more important things. This is what lies behind Jesus' promise that only by losing your life will you find it (Mt. 10:39).

INSTANT GRATIFICATION

Our individualistic culture puts a high premium on the gratification of every desire. We want what we want when we want it; usually we want it right now. The world of commerce constantly reminds us that we have an unqualified right to satisfy our every appetite. The world of instant mass communication turns its heavy guns on us to stimulate those appetites, so that we are almost required to want more and more all the time.

Television commercials, newspaper and magazine advertisements, easy credit, and a bewildering array of products designed to make us look good, feel good, smell good; products designed to give us good flavors and good sounds, ease and comfort—all of these conspire to convince us that the good life is a matter of making the right purchases. At the same time they undercut our capacity for sustained effort, self-discipline, and self-sacrifice.

One striking product of the cult of instant gratification is the "fan." The fan is passive. The fan craves entertainment not participation—or rather, participation by proxy. Under the impact of fandom, sports have become show biz, with winning the only suitable climax. You don't have to play the game or even know anything about it. You identify with your team by buying an imitation team jersey with your hero's number on it. At the championship games it is the fans who shout, "We're number one! "

Pop music fans buy records, pay hefty prices to attend

overcrowded concerts, collect posters of the superstars and imitate not their musical achievements but their hair and dress styles. Fans play records, not instruments, because to play an instrument with any skill you have to practice, and everybody knows practice is "no fun."

Because we demand instant gratification, we no longer save up to buy things the way our parents did. We buy first and pay later so that we do not have to wait or set priorities for ourselves. Thanks to instant credit, we can have everything instantly. Most Americans would consider it unthinkable to do without something they want merely because they cannot afford it.

The moral issue raised by the cult of instant gratification is a difficult one to state. There is nothing inherently evil in sports, pop music, or entertainment itself. The evil arises when we become dependent on these things, when we cannot do without them, when we allow our lives to be shaped by forces outside ourselves. When we can get whatever we want whenever we want it, when we can avoid all pain and struggle, then without ever realizing it, we begin to lose control of our own lives. We lose the capacity for sustained personal effort; we lose the capacity to endure deprivation; we lose the ability to postpone present pleasure for the sake of future good.

When that happens, we miss out on some of life's more significant experiences. Even the goods and pleasures get stale in a hurry, leaving us restless and dissatisfied. Instant gratification leaves us without the personal resources to struggle and grow.

Paul was saying something like this when he described his own life in terms of an athlete in training:

> Every athlete exercises self-control in all things. They do it to receive a perishable wreath, but we an imperishable. Well, I do not run aimlessly, I do not box as one beating the air, but I pommel my body and subdue it, lest after preaching to others I myself should be disqualified (1 Cor. 9:25–27).

This perspective undergirds the ascetical tradition in Christianity. In some ages, that tradition has been dominant;

in others, it has been neglected. Most Americans regard asceticism with faint embarrassment. It smells like Puritanism, the neurotic denial of the world and the good things in it.

A reaffirmation of Christian asceticism does not mean, however, that we have to opt for the excesses of the Puritan temperament. It does not mean that Christians should renounce the genuinely good things of life. Anglicans have always stood within the world-affirming tradition of Christianity; that commitment needs to be maintained.

The strength of the ascetical tradition is its implicit protest against selfishness, acquisitiveness, and competitive striving. It calls us to self-discipline that will enable us to take responsible control of our own lives. It can free us from the pressures of a culture that has brought consumption to the brink of self-destructiveness.

We can cultivate a certain skepticism about the claims and promises dished out by the hucksters of the mass media. We can learn to sit loose to the trivial goods and pleasures that we are constantly told we cannot do without. We can achieve a balance in our lives, yielding neither to the hard sell of the pleasure peddlers nor the contrary temptation of joyless world-renunciation. We can take responsibility for the way we use our time, our energy, our money, testing every choice by our commitment to live an authentic and responsible life before the God who is the source of that life.

FAITH AND HEALTH

Your body can tell a great deal about you. When you "sit up and take notice," your body is saying that you are actively involved in what is going on. When you yawn and fidget, squirm and doze, your body is saying that you are bored to death. Conversely, your treatment of your body says something about your deepest convictions. The slogan of the high-liver—"Live fast, die young, and leave a good-looking corpse"—captures the profound cynicism of those for whom life has no meaning or significance.

By contrast, Christians believe that taking care of our bodies is a religious obligation. How are we supposed to do that? Obviously, we should not abuse our bodies, but we should not coddle ourselves either. We humans, apparently, function best when we do not have it too good. We need nourishing food, of course, but overnourishment is hazardous to our health. Simple foods, we are beginning to learn, are best for the body.

Most religions have advocated fasting as a spiritual discipline. In our society, people diet rather than fast, and they do it for cosmetic rather than spiritual purposes. Dieting can be joyless and monotonous, but fasting is a different matter. We fast only at specific times and seasons; at other times, we are called to feast instead. We ought to be able to do both with equal enthusiasm, as gourmet-theologian Robert Capon has suggested: "When you fast, FAST; and when you eat, EAT." The rhythm of both activities can save us from gluttony and from compulsive calorie counting.

In passing, let it be noted that there is no inherent superiority in either weight or food intake. Thin is not necessarily more commendable than fat. Obesity can be a moral issue when it springs from compulsive eating, or from simple greed. Otherwise, people should be able to affirm their own body types without suffering condemnation by other people with smaller waistlines.

Our freedom from physical labor presents us with similar spiritual hazards. One of the greatest achievements of our technological society is the extent to which it has freed us from brute labor. The increased power available to each of us, even with the increased cost of energy, makes it possible for us to expend less and less physical energy every year.

But this sedentary form of life has its own hazards. We are discovering that the relaxed comfort of our physical surroundings is unhealthy. Most of us do not get enough exercise and our bodies literally waste away as the years go by. The body can cope with fatigue fairly well; it copes less well with stress, to which we are ever more frequently subjected.

Fortunately many people in recent years have come to realize the extent of their deprivation. As a result, the nation has gone on an exercise binge. Exercise has become fashionable. Walking, running, tennis, health clubs, calisthenics, TV exercise programs all serve to affirm the value of physical exercise. We will no doubt reap even more benefits when we learn to build physical activity into our daily lives: using our automobiles less, walking more, throwing away some of our more exotic labor-saving appliances.

Our rediscovery of the value of exercise is a positive good. But like all good things, it breeds its own contradictions and distortions. The cultivation of one's own body can become idolatrous. One physical fitness fanatic was quoted recently as saying, "You have to take care of your body. It's all you have." Thus an activity that, for the Christian, can be a conscientious form of stewardship can also be distorted into a form of self-preoccupation, just as a legitimate concern for good health can become the obsession known as hypochondria.

Once again, then, we are driven back to the recognition of the importance of what we believe and the reasons for what we do. Many of these activities are morally neutral. The meaning of the act depends upon the convictions that underlie it, the motives that inspire it, the intentions that shape it.

For the Christian, the body is a temple of the Holy Spirit. Therefore we will take good care of it. We will seek to keep it under control, because it is God's gift to us and we would use our bodies in the ways that God intends. We were bought for a price and we would not want that sacrifice to be wasted.

The Conventional Vices

At an earlier time, the discussion of Christian behavior would have focused on certain vices: drinking, smoking, gambling. In some circles even dancing, card playing, and movies would have been condemned as "worldly amusements." We have largely rejected such prohibitions because we have regarded them as petty and meaningless. That rejection may have been premature; perhaps the time has come for us to reassess our attitude toward some of these matters, not in the spirit of the killjoy but in frank recognition of the consequences of our behavior for ourselves and for others as well.

ALCOHOL: PROHIBITION AND TEMPERANCE

The crusade against the use of alcoholic beverages is one of the most persistent features of the American religious scene. It is an oft-told story. Church members launched a temperance movement which later changed its emphasis from temperance to total abstinence. Though working first by persuasion, the movement soon changed its tactic to working for laws to forbid the use of alcoholic beverages. The movement reached its zenith with the adoption of the Eighteenth Amendment to the Constitution in 1919, which ushered in the era of national prohibition, the "noble experiment."

Some reform was surely in order, but Prohibition was strong medicine. Americans were the hardest drinkers on the face of the earth. Foreign visitors frequently reported, with awe and amazement, that an American would reach for his whiskey jug the first thing on rising in the morning, even before breakfast. It is no accident that our first major internal conflict was the Whiskey Rebellion, a protest against a measure to tax whiskey.

The effects of prohibition were ambiguous. We have all heard that prohibition touched off a decade of bathtub gin, bootlegging, speakeasies, gangsters—the Roaring Twenties, in brief. The conventional wisdom maintains that, since alcohol was "forbidden fruit," many people, especially the young, began drinking when otherwise they would not have.

That may (or may not) be true, but it is also true that, even long after the repeal of prohibition in 1933, we had not returned to the high level of alcoholic consumption that had been reached before prohibition. Also, when alcohol came back, it did so under many severe restrictions, most of which had not previously existed.

Alcohol made its biggest comeback after World War II as our postwar affluence increased the amount and kind of drinking. Scotch and bourbon replaced the cheaper blended whiskies. The martini reigned supreme. Business, government, and university ran on alcohol. Lush lunches, cocktail parties, receptions, meetings—all were well oiled, but not by oil.

Restrictions on the use of alcohol began to break down. Liquor by the drink became universally available; Sunday drinking spread. Churches that opposed drinking were no longer attacked; they were merely dismissed as "uncool." Drinking became pervasive in American society.

The results of this development were predictable. Alcoholism is now a major health problem. Alcohol is involved in fully half of our fatal automobile accidents. Excessive drinking often results in poor work performance; it sometimes leads to mental illness.

The Episcopal Church was never prominently involved in the prohibition movement. Most Episcopalians have accepted wine as a gift of God, to be used with thanksgiving. The wine of the Eucharist serves as a symbol of God's blessing on the fruit of the vine.

As a result, it has been easy to identify the Episcopal Church as "the drinking man's church" and the Gospel as liberation from petty rules such as "Don't drink." Friend and foe alike have tirelessly repeated witticisms about "whiskey-palians" and stale jokes like, "Wherever there are four Episcopalians, there is sure to be a fifth." Episcopalians have taken a perverse pride in such remarks, which seemed to testify to the sophistication of the church and its freedom from petty moralism.

But less often mentioned is the price of it all. Alcohol produces a major portion of the pastoral problems of most parish clergy. Alcoholism among the clergy is itself a major issue. The use of alcohol has increased in the life of the church itself. Parish meetings, diocesan events, conferences, and other occasions almost always include a "happy hour," when drinks are served. It has come to be *de rigueur* to include alcohol in any ecclesiastical social function.

It seems clear that, as a people, Americans drink too much. We create a climate in which others are encouraged to drink and to increase their drinking. Our overuse of alcohol brings unnecessary grief to ourselves and others. Perhaps we can defend that use but, in the light of its consequences, the burden of proof must rest upon the user.

At the very least, we can scale down our consumption of

alcohol if it seems to be getting to be a problem. We can substitute wines for liquor. We can offer attractive nonalcoholic alternatives when we entertain. We can abstain from alcohol for particular periods. We could even risk our reputation for sophistication by entertaining without alcohol. If you have a problem in your own use of alcohol, your most responsible decision would be to face the fact and, if necessary, to get professional help to deal with it.

As a nation, we seem to be getting over our post prohibition drinking binge. In some sophisticated circles, it has become stylish to cut down on drinking. The Episcopal Church may be able to exercise some leadership in this direction. Since it has never been identified with prohibition or total abstinence, and since it has done much to make drinking respectable in religious circles, the Episcopal Church can perhaps do as much to make nondrinking respectable once more. One need not make a case for teetotalism, but there is a case to be made for temperance and restraint in the use of something that turns out to be both a gift from God and a hazard to health.

DRUG ABUSE

Narcotic substances of one sort or another have been on the scene for a long time, but for the most part their use has been confined to relatively small and isolated groups in the society: the urban poor, immigrants, jazz musicians, the occasional physician who gets hooked on morphine. For the past twenty years, however, we have seen a militant drive to encourage the use of drugs as a way of expanding the mind, of encountering a higher level of reality.

The moral issues involved in the use of such substances are similar to those involved in the use of alcohol. In both cases, use of the substance can create dependency, robbing the self of its freedom. Both can be destructive of physical and mental health. In both cases, one's individual behavior can have tragic consequences for others in one's life: family, friends, coworkers.

Society, however, treats drugs differently from the way it

treats alcohol. We have given up the attempt to prohibit the use of alcohol, but still prohibit the use of marijuana, along with such drugs as morphine, cocaine, and heroin as well as the more esoteric chemicals like LSD and PCP. There has been, for some years, a spirited debate over whether marijuana use should be made legal.

Four arguments are adduced in favor of legalizing marijuana. Tests indicate that marijuana may be no more dangerous than alcohol. If marijuana were legal, users would be shielded from contact with pushers of more dangerous drugs which would still be illegal. The government could control the quality of legal marijuana, protecting users from contamination by toxic substances. Finally, if marijuana were legalized, the government would reap huge benefits from taxes, which are now evaded by illegal operators.

These arguments are persuasive, if not entirely convincing. Those who oppose legalization argue that it would encourage greater use of marijuana, especially by the young. Not everyone agrees that marijuana has been proven safe; the experimental data is sparse and rather inconclusive. Finally, if marijuana were legal, it would probably be marketed by the same kind of sophisticated advertising techniques that have made us a nation of tobacco smokers.

Young people claim, with some justification, that in the past, so-called experts exaggerated the danger of marijuana. As a result, they are inclined to disregard any warnings about the dangers of any drug. Nevertheless the issue is sensitive, precisely because so many young people are lured into the use of dangerous drugs whose dangers they do not understand.

Recent research indicates that marijuana may be more dangerous in the long run than its users realize. It is undeniably hazardous for adolescents who are in an especially vulnerable state of personal development. Marijuana encourages passivity, makes it hard for young persons to concentrate, and inhibits their ability to cope with stressful mental activity or interpersonal relationships. If criminal sanctions are removed from marijuana use, some means will have to be found to discourage its use by the young.

Beyond the matter of dangerous drug abuse is a deeper moral issue in our whole society's casual use of chemicals in order to provide a short cut to health, beauty, and a good night's sleep. When advertising exalts the use of legal drugs to provide for our minds and bodies, it is easy to see how young people can be seduced by the claims of "mind expanding" drugs. It is even easier to see why young people in poor urban neighborhoods turn to hard drugs as a way of escaping an unbearable environment, however briefly and at whatever cost.

Obviously the Christian moral presumption is against the use of potentially harmful drugs. Of course we would recommend extreme caution in approaching them. But what can be done about drug abuse? Since it is irrational behavior to begin with, it is difficult to see how a user is going to be reasoned out of the habit. Caution, likewise, is a difficult attitude to convey to young people who are convinced that they are indestructible.

In many communities, church groups have sponsored drug abuse programs that seek to help people over their dependency on dangerous drugs. Such projects can convey to the drug user the loving concern of the Christian community and can offer resources to enable them to cope with their own problems. Beyond that, when someone close to us develops a drug dependency, rather than sitting in judgment upon them, we can surround them with care and support. If we ourselves should fall victim to drug dependency, we can seek for personal support and professional help in the Christian community.

THE SMOKING CONTROVERSY

While tobacco smoking is not nearly so serious an issue as drugs or alcohol, it confronts us with similar moral questions. Down through the years many traditional Protestant groups have frowned on smoking, but there has never been a major crusade to make it illegal. Since the sale of cigarettes is forbidden to minors, young people regard smoking as something like a rite of passage, a sign that one is now big enough to participate in real, grown-up vices.

Advertising has been largely responsible for making tobacco smoking a major phenomenon in American culture. Smoking has been pictured as an indispensable adjunct to the stylish life, or as part of the total life of the outdoor "he man." We have already seen how the ads that featured the attractive, sophisticated woman with a cigarette have made smoking acceptable behavior for women. "You've come a long way, Baby," the ad chortles. So have the tobacco companies, as today nearly as many women as men have become regular smokers.

But antismoking forces have received massive aid and comfort from an unexpected source. The United States Surgeon General has reluctantly reported that cigarette smoking is statistically associated with a high incidence of lung cancer. Later reports indicate that it contributes to heart and other lung diseases as well. As a result, cigarette commercials have been banned from the air waves, while cigarette ads and packaging are required to carry a warning that smoking may be harmful to your health.

Nonsmoking is now back in style and nonsmokers have risen up to put smokers on the defensive. Air lines are now required to provide nonsmoking areas on every flight. Smoking is prohibited in many public buildings. Restaurants sometimes offer nonsmoking areas.

Now that it has become fashionable to give up smoking, a whole new industry has grown up, claiming the ability, for a fee, to help people kick the habit. It is the difficulty of stopping that highlights the moral dimension of the smoking habit.

With the health hazards involved in smoking reasonably well known and well documented, the Christian moral presumption would be against smoking. Still, the decision must be made by the individual involved. There is no justification for moralistic pressure being brought to bear on smokers by nonsmokers, especially the militant ex-smoker. It is reasonable to let smokers know when their smoking causes discomfort or distress. Beyond that measure of self-protection, nonsmokers have no right to second guess the moral choice made by the person who, having considered the risks, still elects to continue smoking for the sake of the pleasure it provides.

GAMBLING

Gambling has a long history in this country, going back to horse racing, cock fighting, turkey shoots, and public lotteries in the Colonial period. For most of our national history, however, it has been forbidden by law, except under stringently controlled conditions.

For a long time Nevada was the only state to permit casino gambling. The incredible success of the gaming tables of Las Vegas has led to the introduction of gambling to older resorts such as Atlantic City. Gambling has become respectable. Even more, it has become a flourishing business, showing up as a growth stock on the New York Stock Exchange.

The general attitude of the public seems to be, "People are always going to gamble, so why not make it legal and tax it, using the money for legitimate public purposes?" In that spirit, a number of states now operate public lotteries, while New York operates its own system of off-track betting.

Churches opposed these new laws when they were first proposed, but in most instances they have lost the battle to prevent the introduction of legalized gambling. Today gambling is so widely accepted that newspapers regularly carry the current betting odds on weekly football games. Despite religious scruples, gambling, it would seem, has become a part of the American way of life.

And why not? Why not remove the legal restrictions from practices that many people find unobjectionable? When gambling is legal, only those who approve of it need to participate in it. Those opposed can simply decline to gamble. Even if the state itself runs a lottery, what is wrong with that if the money is used for good causes?

Well, a funny thing happened on the way to the lottery.

During the debates on state lotteries, ambitious claims were often made concerning the amount of money to be made for the state. The lottery would support the schools, pay the deficit, and still make it possible to lower taxes because there were, presumably, millions upon millions of people out there just waiting to gamble their money away.

Things have not turned out exactly that way. The income from most state lotteries is far below expectations and I am willing to bet that it will continue to be. Gambling fever does not seem to run as high as we once thought, at least not as far as state lotteries are concerned.

The next step could have been predicted. The state-operated gambling enterprises now engage in heavy advertising to promote their wares. Maryland sponsors TV spots that proclaim, "You have to play to win!" New York advertises Off-Track Betting in billboards and subway ads that cry out, "Get a horse! "

While we may concede that it is legitimate for the state to take advantage of our human weaknesses, it is quite different when the state uses its prestige and its resources to act as a pusher, to lead people into gambling who might not otherwise have been tempted.

In what way does gambling violate the Christian demand to love, or even the Christian obligation to take reasonable care of oneself? After all, it is merely a form of amusement. You could spend a day at the races, pay your admission, buy refreshments, bet on every race, and lose all your money without spending much more than you might at some other form of amusement. If you can afford to spend the money and you enjoy the day, what is wrong?

Nothing is wrong with that. But that situation does not describe the way most gamblers gamble. There is a compulsive element in gambling that makes it dangerous because it so easily gets out of hand. Anyone associated with a serious gambler will tell you that the lure of easy winning quickly overcomes all reason, all argument, all caution. Many a family has fallen into financial ruin because a parent has become hooked on gambling. Gambling constitutes what traditional

moral theology called "an occasion of sin." It can be dangerously habit forming and the victim seldom realized its power
until it is too late.

For most people, gambling never reaches this stage. Participating in the office football pool is certainly an innocuous
form of amusement. A weekly fifty-cent lottery ticket is
hardly the road to perdition. But it is important to know what
we are doing and what the costs may be. American society is
developing toward gambling a rather casual and sentimental
attitude which needs to be reexamined if we are to be serious
in our commitment to live according to the law of love and
the responsible use of ourselves and our resources.

The Corporate Dimensions
of Individual Choices

The issues we have been discussing are intensely personal
because they affect how we choose to live our own lives, use
our own bodies, make our own choices. They have their social dimension, however, for we do not live to ourselves
alone. We have seen how society shapes our moral choices,
whether in a general sort of way by creating a certain moral
climate, or in more specific ways like the promotional advertising that leads us to spend our time and money in a particular fashion.

At the same time, our personal choices have social consequences. My decision to gamble, for example, helps to create
a social climate favorable to gambling and may lead others to
take it up. If I serve drinks in my home, I lend respectability
to drinking and may lead others to indulge.

Moreover, if I become addicted to any of these substances
or activities, I will affect the lives of those about me. If my
health suffers or my personality deteriorates, my family, my
friends, and my coworkers will have to pay some of the price.
In making decisions about my personal life, I cannot leave
these people out of consideration.

At the same time, those people constitute a source of
health, strength, and healing power. If I should become
overwhelmed by addiction to one of the conventional vices, if

I lose the capacity to help myself, I am not therefore alone. I can reach out for help and support to those who care about me.

All of us, at one time or another, need help in coping with the cares and burdens of our personal lives. Christian humility is that virtue which enables us to see ourselves as we really are, with all our limitations and shortcomings. It can enable us to ask for help and support when we need it. Pride closes us off from the possibility of help from other people; humility opens us up to it. In the fellowship of the Christian community, we get by with a little help from our friends. Love dictates that we give them the chance to be helpful.

· 6 ·

Human Sexuality

This is a particularly difficult moment in history in which to make a coherent statement of the Christian sex ethic. Society has an enormous investment in the character of sexual behavior: what is approved, what is tolerated, what is beyond the pale. Our own society is particularly confused about the whole matter of sexuality. We are not even clear about what the word itself means.

Sex in Contemporary Society

The reasons for this unique situation can be summed up in the journalistic phrase, "the sexual revolution." Within our own century, our knowledge about sexual matters, our attitude toward sex, and our sexual behavior, have all undergone vast changes. In the process, Christian teaching about sexual matters has often seemed destructive, irrelevant, or downright quaint.

The behavioral sciences, along with biology, have contributed to our increased knowledge of sexuality. Perhaps the most significant contribution was Sigmund Freud's recognition of the centrality and the pervasiveness of sex in human personality. For Freud, libido is that primal energy that drives a person toward ultimate sexual union with another. But libido is also the source of self-love, of love for parents and friends, of the impulse toward generosity and self-sacrifice. Thus broadly conceived, sex is at the very core of our humanity.

It is a misuse of language, therefore, to speak of sex merely as genital activity. To "have sex" or "not to have sex" is not a human possibility. We are sexual beings; our sexuality affects how we see the world, how we respond to it, and how we live in it.

In the individual person, humanity is incomplete. When God created man in his own image, he created both male and female. The fullness of humanity requires both; either one is incomplete without the other. "Man" and "woman" describe alternative ways of being human, each possessing its own unique possibilities and making its unique contributions to the human enterprise. Man and woman together, in concourse and fellowship, supplement each other, together constituting that full humanity which is the image of God.[1]

THE SEXUAL REVOLUTION

The most significant contribution toward the sexual revolution has been the development of contraceptives: safe, effective, inexpensive, and generally available. By reducing the likelihood that sexual intercourse will result in an unwanted pregnancy, contraception removes one of the major social controls from sexual activity.

The worldwide population explosion has contributed to our sexual attitudes by making procreation less important. When the future of the human race was precarious, when more than half of all newborn infants died early, it was necessary for all members of the community to contribute to the continuation of the people. Marriage was expected of all able-bodied adults, and large families were highly valued. Neither are necessary today, so the value of both has declined.

Venereal disease has always been one of the major risks of casual sexual encounters. Since World War II, antibiotics have proved impressively effective against the most common of these diseases. As a result, the fear of venereal disease is no longer the deterrent to sexual promiscuity that it once was.

Along with these developments, the attitude of society toward sexual intercourse has drastically changed. The value traditionally ascribed to virginity has declined. Pleasure, rather than procreation, has become the central value in sexual intercourse. A rather superficial reading of Freud has led many to believe that it is unhealthy for people to control their sexual appetites, that sexual intercourse is a therapeutic release of sexual tension. Society has become more indulgent, less likely to punish or ostracize those who depart from traditional norms of sexual behavior.

In the meantime, sex has been brought out into the open. While we were once afraid to talk about sex, now we seem to feel compelled to talk about it. Major magazines regularly carry articles on sexual technique. Erotic books appear on the best-seller lists. The bulk of this literature does not support the view of America as a sexually freed-up society. It seems that as sex has come out of the closet it has brought with it an assortment of new demands, new expectations, and new anxieties. The consuming public now has to be instructed in how to behave—and even how to misbehave.

The Christian Sexual Tradition

In this changing climate, the Christian tradition has not offered much help. While the Bible has some things to say about sex, that subject was not a major interest of the biblical writers. Their observations about sexuality were usually made in the context of some other matter. The Christian community, on the other hand, has at times seemed to be excessively concerned with sex, often acting as though sex were an invention of the devil.

OLD TESTAMENT TREATMENT

In the Old Testament, marriage and family life are not argued for; they are taken for granted. Polygamy existed in Israel's early years, without any disapproval voiced, but it disappears later. The integrity of family life is safeguarded by laws against adultery and a provision requiring that when a man dies without children his brother should father children by his widow.

The place of women was ambivalent; they were valued as wives and mothers, but were still regarded as property. It was unlawful to seduce a virgin because then she was spoiled goods and could not command a good price in the marriage market. Adultery was a crime against property, more serious when the offense was against a husband than when the wife was wronged.

Nevertheless, the Jews did hold sexuality in high regard. One evidence for this observation is the Song of Solomon which, though spiritualized by centuries of interpretation, is still a frank celebration of erotic love and its pleasures.

NEW TESTAMENT WITNESS

Jesus exhibits an entirely new attitude toward women. He mingled freely with them, included them among his disciples, allowed them to listen to his teaching, and even had them accompany him on his travels. The Gospels agree that his first resurrection appearance was to women, though his male disciples found it hard to credit their witness.

Paul has been accused of antipathy toward women, but his views seem fairly consistent with his era. He requires women to keep their heads covered and warns them against speaking in church, but these admonishments would have been quite conventional at the time. He suggests that it is better to stay unmarried, as he himself apparently was, but that view can be understood as part of his expectation that the world was shortly coming to an end. His later epistles, in the usual Jewish fashion, take marriage and family life for granted.

Paul could also make quite revolutionary statements about the place of women in the church. "There is neither Jew nor Greek," he wrote, "There is neither slave nor free, there is neither male nor female; for you are all one in Christ Jesus" (Gal. 3:18). He mentions women as well as men among the fellow workers he wishes to greet in the cities where he has labored. Thus the New Testament opens up the possibility of an entirely new relationship between the sexes, one based on equality, mutuality, and freedom.

THE CHRISTIAN ERA

But the power of culture soon asserted itself and, by the fifth century, most of those possibilities had dimmed. It is not true to say that the early fathers of the church foisted off onto the world a peculiarly antagonistic attitude toward sex. They merely shared the view of sex, and of women, that was characteristic of their time. That era was permeated with philosophical dualism that set the body against the spirit and advocated a rigorous subjection of the flesh.[2]

The church fathers exalted virginity as the most Christlike way of life. Since not all men were capable of maintaining the virgin state, however, marriage was permissible as a concession to the weakness of the flesh.

Sexual intercourse itself they regarded as abhorrent. They seemed to find it somewhat embarrassing that God should choose such an inappropriate method for preserving the human race. Since intercourse was essential for a married couple to produce offspring, it could not be sinful. But it would be sinful if it were indulged in for mere pleasure.

Some Christian thinkers, of course, have had more positive views of marriage and family life. Clement of Alexandria believed that women are equally endowed with men and share the same human nature. Nevertheless, despite the numbers of truly remarkable women in the Middle Ages who had distinguished careers and reputations, the view persisted that woman is essentially a malformed male who consequently needs to be restrained, protected, and governed.

The Reformation continued to teach the subordination of women, on scriptural and historical grounds. Though the idea of the priesthood of all believers admits of no differences in the sexes, still the reformers believed that woman's special ministry is motherhood and that she should be restricted to the domestic realm.

John Calvin, however, had a more positive view of sexual intercourse. It is instituted by God, he believed, and therefore must be honorable, provided it is engaged in only for procreation. While uneasy about the pleasure of sexual intercourse, he believed that God approved it, provided husband and wife enjoy themselves with modesty and propriety.

In the light of this long history of Christian teaching, it is no wonder that the church in recent years has been somewhat on the defensive about its views of women and sexuality. Although the antisex tradition has not been the only one in Christianity, it has been predominant. The view of women as inferior—or at least subordinate—to man has been so widely accepted as to seem undeniably orthodox. Thus critics of traditional Christian views of sexuality are on rather firm ground when they claim that the church has tended to disapprove of sexual pleasure and to treat women as inferior to men. Both views have been subject to significant revision in recent decades.

Equality for Women

During the past two hundred years, a major movement has sought to improve the position of women in western societies. The movement is based on the conviction that women are equal to men in all important ways and should therefore be accorded equal freedom and opportunity by government, church, and other social institutions.

The traditional place of women in society has been dictated by their childbearing and child-rearing functions. Infant mortality was so high that a woman had to bear many children to insure that some would survive. Women were especially vulnerable to diseases associated with childbirth; their life expectancy was relatively short. Because they tended to be smaller and weaker than men, they could perform only the lighter domestic tasks. Because of the prevalence of violence and danger, women's movements were restricted to times and places where they could be protected.

Those conditions have changed so drastically that our assumptions about women's role in society have been challenged. Infant mortality has been sharply reduced, as has average family size. For many women, childbearing and child rearing are restricted to one segment of a lengthened life span. The stereotype of women as flighty and irrational has been laid to rest by the performance of women on every level of education. Technology has made men's physical strength irrelevant in most occupations.

Women have adopted so many roles and occupations once associated exclusively with men that we are no longer sure just what are the traits and characteristics that can properly be labeled *masculine* or *feminine*. Women can be tough and aggressive, and men can be tender and nurturing.

Despite this uncertainty, we do not seem to be tending toward a "unisex" society in which male-female differences are obliterated. The chasm between man and woman is deep and persisting even though we may not always be sure about what constitutes the difference, aside from the obvious biological ones. Sexuality, at its most profound level, remains a mystery, the deepest mystery of our created humanity.

We do know, however, that the differences between man and woman complement each other, so that our full humanity requires both sexes. Their interaction, collaboration, and fellowship are required for the richness and variety of the human enterprise.

The church has found it difficult to assimilate this move for the equality of women. Unlike the movement for racial equality, in which the church was challenged to live up to its convictions, in this case the church has had to reconsider and revise positions that have been held throughout most of its history.

Opponents of women's equality point to biblical passages that would seem to legitimate inequality. Jesus chose no women as apostles. Paul commands women to keep silent in the church and says that the wife should be subject to the husband. These passages would seem to validate a subordinate position for women in both church and society.

But other passages already referred to—Jesus' treatment of women, Paul's dramatic statement of full human equality— would seem to point the other way. Every age, to be sure, reads Scripture through the presuppositions of its own culture, and our age is no exception. But we have as much right to make interpretations in the light of our experience as did those earlier Christians who emphasized other passages to reach other conclusions. We have improved upon Paul's attitude toward slavery and would make no apologies for that change. Similarly we are now moving beyond Paul's statements concerning woman's subjection to a realization of the full import of his more provocative proclamation about the equality of woman and man.

That movement involves us in a revision of long-held and generally accepted views. It is not easy for a large and diverse community like the church to make such changes in its stance on such a major issue. It is no wonder, then, that matters having to do with the role of women in society should provoke such intensity of debate and controversy.

Ethical Issues in Sexual Encounter

If all encounters between male and female are somehow sexual in nature, the moral question becomes, "What is the proper expression of that sexual dimension?"

There are those who assert that any sexual expression is legitimate if it is grounded in love. This viewpoint fails to take seriously the question of what is appropriate, or fitting, to the particular situation. The almost universal incest taboo, for example, is based on the understanding that those who are most vulnerable should not be available for sexual intercourse. Though sexual union is the ultimate expression of intimacy, it is not fitting within the peculiar intimacy of the relation of parent and child.

The question of fitness is raised for us in a variety of ways because men and women are increasingly thrown together in the world of business, politics, education, and social life as well as in family life. Men and women can be friends, coworkers, business and professional associates, companions in leisure time activities, all without becoming what novelists refer to euphemistically as "lovers." With so many opportunities for association and interaction, men and women need to know just what behavior is appropriate when and with whom.

The Christian presumption is that marriage provides the

proper context for the fullest expression of our sexuality. That presumption does not have to be stated legalistically, as the church has often done. It is not a matter of pronouncing certain words over a couple, thereby making right something that was otherwise wrong. Rather, marriage is the public acknowledgment and acceptance of the relationship within which sexual activity takes its proper place.

Paul offers a theological basis for this presumption when he writes: "Do you not know that he who joins himself to a prostitute becomes one body with her? For, as it is written, 'The two shall become one'" (1 Cor. 6:16). Paul did not explore the implications of that bald statement, but we now know enough about sex and interpersonal relationships that we can apply his insight to the whole realm of sexual relations.

Sexual intercourse is, indeed, the ultimate expression of a genuinely intimate, caring, and loving relationship. But it also helps to establish, enrich, and reinforce that relationship. Paul is saying that this intimate contact establishes a bond whether the partners intend it or not, whether they want it or not. And once established, that bond persists, even though ignored or denied. Thus he warns us not to get involved in such a relationship if we do not intend it to be serious and permanent.

Marriage is a couple's public commitment to sustain and deepen such a relationship. They agree to trust each other privately and to be accountable for that trust publicly. Because each partner in the full sexual union is vulnerable to hurt, disappointment, and exploitation, the commitment to permanent caring and trust is essential to enable each one to take the risks necessary to make their sexual encounter—and their life together—rich, pleasurable, and honest.

The Christian presumption against sex outside marriage has often been stated legalistically. The real judgment, however, is not that such behavior is wicked or degenerate, but that it exposes the parties to hazards that the institution of marriage is intended to avoid.

Traditionally those hazards were such unwanted consequences as pregnancy and venereal disease. Both of these hazards have been reduced, in principle at least, by effective methods of contraception and antibiotics. In practice, of course, both unwanted pregnancies and venereal disease are on the rise, indicating that many couples are either ignorant of the hazards or reckless of the consequences. Thus the case can be made for helping people to understand what they are doing and what they need to do to stay out of trouble.

That is why some people press for sex education in the schools and for the availability of birth-control information for unmarried young people. It is not a matter of accepting the prevailing moral standards, but of helping people to avoid the most disastrous consequences of their actions.

The more subtle hazard of casual sexual intercourse is that it is profoundly self-alienating. Our sexual behavior expresses our deepest feelings and exposes us to deep hurts, while it promises our greatest pleasures. When sexual intercourse is regarded as merely fun, merely a physical exercise that releases tension or provides good feelings without involving the self on its deepest level, at that point it becomes self-alienating.

That is why Christians are inevitably skeptical of casual sexual encounters: prostitution, one-night stands, "swinging," freely available sex. Many people who get involved in such behavior sooner or later begin to see that it leads nowhere and provides no permanent satisfaction and react against it with disgust and self-loathing.

WITHOUT BENEFIT OF CLERGY

Not all sexual intercourse outside marriage is casual or irresponsible. Some couples, in recent years, have chosen to maintain a sexual liaison, even to live together, out of a sense of commitment and caring, trying to be honestly intimate without exploiting one another. Many explicitly resist marriage on the ground that they do not feel prepared for a permanent commitment, or do not believe in the possibility of such a permanent arrangement.[3]

They have some evidence to support this viewpoint. They can see the large number of disastrous marriages around them. Many come from broken homes themselves. Some have themselves lived through a bad marriage and tend to shy away from a repeat performance. They resort to cohabitation as a substitute for marriage, either temporarily or permanently.

The parents and friends of many of these couples regard their arrangements with considerable ambivalence. On the one hand, the idea of couples living together without being married goes against everything they have been taught, so they feel that their standards have been violated. On the other hand, those who have experienced a troubled marriage, or an unsatisfactory sexual relationship in their marriage are inclined to look indulgently on the experiment in the hope that perhaps the couple will benefit by the experience.

Certainly the previous generation has oversold marriage as a cure-all for personal inadequacies and sexual longings. Certainly too, the failure rate of youthful marriages is high enough to warrant the caution of the young. If the choice is between a high risk of marital disaster and a temporary nonmarital liaison, we can surely understand that a couple might make a responsible and conscientious choice for the latter.

The hazard of that choice, however, is that, the better the relationship, the higher the risk. For the relationship is, in fact, an informal, nonlegal marriage of sorts. It is subject to the same pressures, temptations, and frustrations of formal marriage, as well as sharing some of its joys, pleasures, and fulfillments. To paraphrase Paul, when one joins one's body to anyone, the two become one flesh. And when the relationship breaks up, it is just as painful to the participants as the divorce that breaks up a marriage. They feel all of the hurt and suffering, the bitterness and anger, the disappointment and self-doubt that we associate with divorce.

Couples usually enter into these relationships with an agreement: "It's just for now; we have no claim on one another. When it no longer satisfies, we'll break up with no hard feelings."

That is easier said than done. The two may not agree about when the relationship should end. If the relationship becomes deeper, it becomes all the harder to break up. And if one person has a greater investment in the relationship than the other, they have a built-in recipe for disaster. Such liaisons, then, are precarious at best and hazardous for both parties. The tragedy inherent in the situation is the inability of the partners to commit themselves to a sustained relationship without qualification or reservation.

Homosexuality

Homosexuality is currently one of the most controversial issues in Christian ethical discourse. Homosexual behavior is nothing new, of course, but in the past it has been, by general agreement, unmentionable. Now that it has surfaced as a matter for public debate, Christian ethical thinkers can no longer avoid trying to work out a responsible attitude toward it.

Biblical references to homosexual behavior would seem to settle the matter without need for debate. Leviticus sums up the view of the ancient Hebrews: "If a man lies with a male as with a woman, both of them have committed an abomination; they shall be put to death" (20:13).

While the subject is rarely mentioned in the New Testament, Paul seems pretty clear about what he thinks. Among the consequences of ungodliness, he mentions men who ". . . gave up natural relations with women and were consumed with passion for one another" (Rom. 1:27).

But as we have already seen, it is not always helpful to take biblical references literally, without seeing them in the context of their time. Our treatment of homosexuality must be based on our understanding of the basic Christian ethical norm of love, guided by our understanding of the issue itself, in the light of the best information available to us. The growth of new knowledge about homosexuality has produced a new attitude toward it and forced us to reconsider what the church should teach about the matter.[4]

Our knowledge of homosexuality, though growing, is still slight, and much of what we know is in dispute. Homosexuality has been regarded with such indignation that few homosexual people have been willing to volunteer information about themselves. Psychiatrists see only the sick ones. The public hears only about those involved in some scandal or crime. Thus the assumption is easily made that homosexuals are either criminals or neurotics.

More recently, many homosexual persons have, as they say, come out of the closet and declared their condition publicly. They have attempted to assert their own worth, calling on society to accept their behavior by removing laws against their practices and by according them equal rights and privileges. More specifically, they have laid claim to the concern and compassion of the Christian community on the ground that they, too, are beloved children of God, for whom Christ died.

Still the questions about homosexuality remain unanswered. Why do some people become homosexual, while others in similar situations do not? To what extent is homosexuality genetic in origin, to what extent culturally conditioned, to what extent learned behavior? Can homosexuality be cured—and should it be?

It may not be possible to answer these questions categorically because homosexual persons differ from one another as much as the general population. Still, our answers to these questions are bound to shape our understanding of the moral issues that homosexuality raises for us.

Those issues are felt most intently by people who are charged with training and guiding the young. Parents, pastors, and teachers often fear that if homosexuality becomes socially approved as a legitimate way of life, some young people, already somewhat confused about their sexual identity, will be led into directions that they will later regret. They feel especially sensitive about the possibility that the church may do something that would tolerate—or even condone—homosexual behavior.

The church has not yet made any definitive statement about its stand on homosexuality, but some indications of what that stand will be are already discernible.

The Christian moral presumption favors heterosexuality on the ground that God evidently intends humanity to be both male and female in collaboration. Either sex without the other is incomplete. On that basis, homosexuality would be seen as falling short of the fullness of sexual possibility intended by God, an inability to attain the rich and complex intimacy with a member of the opposite sex.

At the same time, we have to recognize that some adults are psychologically disposed to seek sexual outlet with members of their own sex and there is little they can do to change their feelings. Where homosexuality is a condition visited upon a person without his or her consent, that person can hardly be condemned for it. There are, apparently, some few who consciously choose a homosexual orientation, but indications are that such a choice is usually influenced by other factors: rebellion against social norms, or identification with homosexuality as a radical political act.

How should the heterosexual Christian regard the homosexual person? How should such a person be treated by the Christian community? How should the homosexual Christian behave?

First we ought to speak, not of the homosexual, but of the homosexual person for, though our sexuality is at the heart of our personhood, we are always more than just our sexual orientation. No one is "merely" a homosexual; therefore no one should be evaluated solely on the grounds of their homosexual orientation or behavior. The Episcopal Church adopted this view in its 1976 General Convention when it resolved that homosexual persons are to be treated as children of God, entitled to the care, concern, and full ministry of the church.

Second, regardless of our view of homosexuality, we ought to support full civil rights and liberties for homosexual persons. The horror and indignation with which society has treated homosexuality has led to a secretive attitude which makes such persons vulnerable to prosecution, harassment, and even blackmail. Homosexual persons should not be liable to the loss of their jobs, or eviction from their residences. The church should lend its support to the removal of these legal proscriptions and social disabilities.

Third, Christians who do not share their orientation should nevertheless adopt a compassionate attitude toward homosexual persons who are trying conscientiously to work out a satisfying way of life. The most destructive aspect of the homosexual life is the variety of promiscuous and exploitative practices that have grown up in the homosexual subculture: cruising among the gay bars and hangouts, casual and degrading sexual contacts.

Some have attempted to find their way toward more stable, caring relationships, even forming homosexual "marriages." The church cannot go so far as to sanction homosexual marriage because marriage is by definition the union of man and woman. It is, however, possible to see the relative value of stable and caring relationships in contrast to the promiscuity of casual sexual encounters.

Theologian Norman Pittenger maintains that homosexual genital sex can be a fully legitimate expression of interpersonal love that is an outgrowth of the love of God.[5] Few Christian moralists would go so far in approving homosexual behavior, but would rather see it as a tolerable choice which might be the best possibility available to persons in a particular situation.

To define a position on homosexuality, then, is difficult because it must include both a *yes* and a *no*. Christians cannot regard homosexuality as a way of life to be approved and commended to the faithful as a matter of choice. Where it is not a matter of choice, but is simply the way a person is, the present state of our knowledge would indicate that the person's sexuality is in some way circumscribed, less than fully adequate.

But at the same time, Christians will support the conscientious efforts of homosexual persons to make the best possible adjustment to their condition. They are to be loved and accepted like anyone else: as sinners for whom Christ died. There is no warrant for condemnation or discrimination against them.

Sexual Ethics in Perspective

Our society is overly preoccupied with sex. For pop culture, love equals sex. For conventional respectability, morality equals sex. Explicit references to sexual material in film and literature is regarded as frank and daring. Indeed, we take considerable pride in what we regard as our lustiness.

But if we read our Freud correctly, we know that libido, that fundamental drive which is sexual in origin, spills out over all loving and creative activity. Thus sex as popularly conceived is only a small part of a much larger picture. The ethical issues posed by our sexuality are real, but it is easy to overemphasize them. As C. S. Lewis has pointed out, ". . . the centre of Christian morality is not here. . . . The sins of the flesh are bad, but they are the least bad of all sins."[6]

The loss of virginity once made one a "fallen woman." Homosexuals, when discovered, were hounded out of the community. Society acted as though these were the most offensive forms of human sinfulness. Today our mass media are permeated with allusions to sex. Sex is used to sell everything from mouth wash to boiler plate. Individuals and groups engage in the most diverse kinds of sexual experimentation, often at the top of their voice. In such a climate, it is not surprising that some people will be led to do things they should not do, that they hurt themselves and others, that they program themselves into behavioral games that are futile and destructive.

At least the personal and social costs of such behavior can be reduced. Then perhaps we can view such matters in a more realistic perspective, seeing some sexual lapses as foolish rather than wicked, calling forth a response of regret rather than outrage.

It is hardly necessary to restate the obvious fact that we live at a time of considerable sexual experimentation of all sorts. Some, to be sure, is the product of self-indulgence, exhibiting a callous and exploitative attitude toward other people, or a pointless search for thrills and kicks. But some is motivated by an honest striving for intimacy with integrity, in a context of caring, loving relationships. In that search, our conventional norms of behavior may, incidently, be violated or disregarded.

Many of those efforts are doomed to failure. Mistakes will be made, people hurt, lives blighted. But the results may not be all negative. We may, in the process, learn something new about the nature of human sexuality, about the extent and the limits of our freedom and accountability.

That being the case, then perhaps we ought to exercise great restraint in the passing of judgment, as Jesus commanded us to do. We need not be either naïve or sentimental about such matters. We are free to voice our own convictions regarding the behavior of those around us. But if our attitude is worthy of the Gospel, it will be characterized by sensitivity and compassion, rather than judgmental moralism.

A corresponding responsibility is laid upon those who engage in such experimentation. Some people feel that they have discovered ways of living that are superior to the failures and hypocrisies involved in conventional sexual and marital standards. But even if they are convinced they are right, they still need to maintain a decent respect for the opinions of others and not flaunt their unconventional behavior in ways that will shock people whose views are more conventional.

When Paul asserted his freedom from conventional standards (for him the issue was eating meat that had been offered to idols), he expressed his concern that his behavior not offend the brother whose conscience dictated different behavior (1 Cor. 8). That advice is still valuable, for if we are to coexist as one united people within a dynamic, pluralistic society with changing rules and standards, we need to respect and care for one another, especially those with whom we differ the most.

· 7 ·

Marriage and Family Life

Marriage is a universal human institution. It exists in every society, in every age. Can we, then, speak in any meaningful sense of *Christian marriage*? If by that term is meant something unique and exclusive, something significantly different from marriage as other human communities conceive it, then the answer must be *No*. But the answer is *Yes* if we mean merely that the Christian community maintains a particular view of marriage, even though it may be shared by many outside the Christian fold. Christians look at marriage from the perspective of certain presumptions about what marriage ought to be.

We have to concede that our view of marriage is historically conditioned. It has changed with time, mostly for the better, we believe. At one time, the marriage partner was selected by the parents; women especially had little choice about who their mate would be. The fundamental bond of marriage was not love but faithfulness which, it was hoped, would ultimately grow into love with the passage of time. Marriage was an alliance of families, sealed by contract and accompanied by payments and promises.

In previous ages, the husband dominated the marriage. The wife was his property; no outside agency could interfere with his treatment of her. She could own no property in her own right. In many countries she had no independent legal existence.

In its early years, the church took a rather dim view of marriage, as it did of all matters related to sex. The church fathers, to be sure, did acknowledge that marriage was ordained by God for the procreation of children and the perpetuation of the race, but marriage was a subordinate good. Virginity was the highest good, but since, as Paul put it, "It is better to marry than to be aflame with passion" (1 Cor. 7:9), marriage served as a "remedy for concupiscence," a legitimate context for accommodating man's sexual needs.

Christian Presumptions Concerning Marriage

Most of us today find these older views of marriage quaint, if not revolting. It is clear, then, that our view of Christian marriage has undergone some change. Some of our presumptions about marriage have also changed, while others have remained constant through the ages. These presumptions are summed up in the Declaration of Intention which is to be signed by anyone who seeks to be married in the Episcopal Church. They include the following:

> We hold marriage to be a lifelong union of husband and wife. . . . We believe it is for the purpose of mutual fellowship, encouragement and understanding, for the procreation (if it may be) of children, and their physical and spiritual nurture, and for the safeguarding and benefit of society.[1]

PERMANENCE

The Christian presumption is that marriage is intended to be permanent. This view is an outgrowth of the biblical teaching that in marriage the man and the woman have been made one flesh. Paul's observation that if anyone joins his body to a harlot they become one flesh (1 Cor. 6:16) bears witness to the fact that sexual union creates and strengthens a deep and lasting bond between man and woman. It symbolizes and celebrates that bond at the same time. Marriage is the public act by which a man and a woman declare their intention to create and preserve such a bond. By committing themselves to one another in a permanent, unconditional, unqualified, and unreserved union—for better or for worse—they create a climate of security and stability within which the full range of sexual interaction and union can take place.

Since we are at our most vulnerable, most open to hurt and failure, in our sexual interaction, the security of permanence is necessary to enable the full flowering of the deepest kind of interpersonal and sexual relationship. Thus the Christian community declared itself opposed to any casual "contract of convenience," which is what much of secular society regards marriage to be.

FELLOWSHIP

Anglicanism early recognized that interpersonal relationship is one of the most significant aspects of marriage. The earliest Prayer Books listed "mutual society" as one of the purposes of marriage. Seventeenth-century divines—Jeremy Taylor most notably—extolled the blessings of married love, the "queen of friendships" as Taylor called it. Taylor went on to celebrate the role of sexual intercourse in strengthening the love between husband and wife.[2]

Even the ancient biblical writers recognized that marriage helped to overcome the loneliness of the single life. In Genesis, God looks at Adam and observes, "It is not good that man should be alone" (2:18). Marriage can thus be seen as a testimony to the inherently social character of our humanity. We all need deep and lasting human companionship, intimate and caring relationships.

MUTUALITY

The conviction that the relationship of husband and wife should be founded on mutuality is a rather late development in Christian history. Paul's dictum that "the husband is the head of the wife" (Eph. 5:23) had long been accepted without argument. Not until fairly recently has this standard been challenged and ultimately repudiated. The marriage rite itself signaled the change when the 1928 Book of Common Prayer eliminated the traditional promise of the wife to "love, honor, and obey" her husband. Mutual vows were substituted; both husband and wife thereafter vowed to "love, honor, and cherish" each other.

Mutuality is more than a theory; it sets a standard for equal treatment in the marriage and in running the home. Not surprisingly, men have found it harder to accept this change than have women. Many men still seem to expect their wives to wait on them, pick up their socks, cater to their whims, and make them the center of their lives. Even wives who work full time are often expected to do all of the housework and the cooking. Many men still seem to feel demeaned if called upon to do household tasks.

Mutuality in marriage makes it appropriate for men to wash dishes, do laundry, and clean house. Of course, some division of labor is necessary in every marriage, but in a marriage grounded in mutuality, those decisions will be made together, with neither partner automatically required to perform any particular task—or automatically excluded from it.

On a more significant level, now that women have entered the job market more extensively, we can expect to see more and more family crises when either husband or wife is offered a new job or a promotion that requires a move on the part of the family. In the past, the expectation has always been that the man's job takes precedence and the wife makes the adjustment. Mutuality requires that any such decision be faced and made together, not by one party acting by fiat.

PROCREATION

Christians presume that, ordinarily, a marriage will produce children. A good marriage will provide the context of love, trust, and stability that enables children to grow into healthy and responsible adults. But the procreation of children is no longer seen as the central purpose of marriage. Indeed, many older persons marry long after they have passed the age of childbearing. Some married couples commit themselves to remain childless because they are convinced that the pressures of world population make it incumbent upon some to refrain from bringing more children into the world. Others, often couples with heavy professional agendas or public commitments, may decide to forego parenthood because they know they are not likely to be able to extend to their children the care and attention a growing family requires.

In any case, modern marriage calls for responsible family planning: how many children to have, when to have them, whether to have them at all. These are questions which cannot be left to chance. The Anglican Communion has long been committed to the legitimacy and the value of family planning. As long ago as 1930, the bishops meeting at Lambeth acknowledged the decision to limit the size of one's family as a valid exercise of Christian responsibility. They were, however, exceedingly cautious in their approach to contraception. The 1958 Lambeth Conference went further by declaring that family planning is the moral responsibility of every Christian family.[3]

The availability of contraception does not eliminate the moral considerations in family planning. Couples may limit the size of their families, or even decide to have no children at all, for good and proper reasons. But their decision may also be the result of a tendency toward self-preoccupation, an immature dependence upon one another, or an inordinate concern for property and possessions.

Couples who choose childlessness or very small families should be aware of their need for outlets for their parental and charitable inclinations. They need to discover ways to manifest their concern for other people, their care for the next generation. Otherwise they will end up lavishing their affections upon possessions or pets, many of whom fare better than some children in our society.

SEX

Because of the presumption that marriage offers the only adequate context for the full expression of sexual love, most discussions of sexual morality tend to focus on the issue of sex outside marriage. But the moral dilemmas of sex are not unknown within the married state. Sex can be used as a weapon for the manipulation of the marriage partner. It can be an expression of anger, hostility, resentment, aggression. It can even be a way of evading significant interpersonal issues, as evidenced by those couples who normally settle an argument by going to bed.

Marriage counselors tell us that the quality of sexual adjustment in marriage is usually related to the quality of the interpersonal relationship. Love, trust, caring, openness, and the capacity to forgive and be reconciled are important to the continuing health of the sexual dimension of marriage and are not always easy to maintain.

Because the sexual relationship is so dependent upon the level of trust between the partners, adultery has to be seen as the fundamental betrayal of the marriage partner. Adultery has long been regarded as sinful, as the seventh commandment makes clear, but its meaning has changed somewhat through the centuries.

In the ancient world, adultery was the violation of the man's property rights to the exclusive sexual use of his wife. It raised doubts about the legitimacy of his children and the integrity of his family. But today, marriage is seen more as a personal relationship than as a property arrangement. In that context, adultery becomes even more offensive because it intrudes into the intimate relationship that lies at the very heart of the married state.

Marriage Casualties

Marriage in contemporary society is something of a perilous journey. Since we live so much longer today, marriage has to be of a more enduring quality. Because our society is so dynamic, we tend to undergo more significant personal changes than did most people of earlier times. As a result, couples often grow apart rather than more closely together. At the same time we have been led to build up grossly unrealistic expectations about marriage—what it ought to be, what it can do for us—and then we are disappointed when life fails to measure up to the dream.

So it is not surprising that many marriages are in trouble. Couples often find it impossible to maintain the constant close communication that enables them to stay in touch with one another through the complex and manifold changes of life. Marriage today takes considerable effort in looking at, facing, talking about, and working on the quality of the interpersonal relationship itself.

When it appears that trouble is looming on the horizon, couples may need to seek professional help. When that happens, they are well advised to find a counselor who shares the Christian view of marriage, one who will see the marriage relationship itself as the client. Many marriage counselors today are more committed to the secular value of individual self-fulfillment and are unable or unwilling to help couples face and deal with the stresses and tensions in their relationship. It is always easier to advise the abandonment of the relationship in the hope that something better will turn up.

DIVORCE

Despite the best and most conscientious efforts of a couple to salvage a troubled marriage, divorce sometimes seems to be the most responsible decision. But if marriage is seen as a permanent union, how can divorce be sanctioned, or even tolerated?

The church has had great difficulty with this issue from its earliest days. On the one hand, Jesus' pronouncement on the matter (Mk. 10:2–10) would seem to make divorce impossible, though Matthew's version admits unchastity as a ground for divorce (Mt. 19:3–9). On the other hand, since some marriages clearly should be dissolved, throughout most of its history the church has permitted divorce under certain extreme conditions, but has usually refused to permit the remarriage of divorced persons.

After 1946, the Episcopal Church permitted the remarriage of a divorced person, but only when a bishop pronounced the judgment that no true Christian marriage had existed in the first place. While this canonical provision was moderately serviceable, it put the emphasis on a legalistic, rather than on a pastoral approach to divorce. It also put the emphasis, not on divorce, but on remarriage.

This provision also rested on the curious and rather dubious theological proposition that a true Christian marriage is indissoluble whereas another, presumably more ordinary marriage, may be dissolved. It was the anomaly caused by this contradiction that finally led the 1973 General Convention to adopt a new canon which explicitly recognized the termination of a marriage and the right of the partners to be remarried with the blessing of the church.[4]

How can that decision be reconciled with the traditional Christian commitment to the permanence of the marriage bond? Many people have raised this question, some even accusing the church of abandoning traditional moral standards and accommodating itself to the lax standards of an era that has no idea of what the church means by Christian marriage.

It is certainly true that divorce has become widespread in our society, to the extent that some social critics have said that America practices serial monogamy—only one wife at a time. We would have to concede that many couples rush headlong into divorce the moment conflict or dissatisfaction appear in their marriage.

The answer to these critics is that the church does not sanction a casual or neutral attitude toward divorce. Christians do intend their marriages to be permanent and are obligated to make every effort to achieve that permanence. Nevertheless it is clear that, at all times and places, some marriages have ended in disaster. There is no moral superiority in requiring a couple to continue living together long after the disappearance of the love and faithfulness that bound them together.

The Christian moral presumption in favor of the permanence of marriage places the burden of proof on the person who would make a case for getting a divorce. Still that case can be made under some conditions. Just as Christians make a presumption in favor of peace and against war, we can envision situations in which the decision to go to war is both valid and responsible.

Most of us know people who have gone through a divorce.

At best it is painful and perilous. Few conscientious people make that decision easily. The original marriage relationship is a real one, even when it has become distorted and destructive. Shedding a husband or wife is like losing a limb. It is a profound and violent trauma that may take years to heal. And even though society no longer relegates divorced persons to a life of isolation and contempt, still a divorce is perceived as a failure, one that is inevitably shared by both partners, although one may seem more obviously guilty than the other.

The painfulness of that process may be the best safeguard to insure that divorce will not be resorted to as a way of evading hard choices in a marriage. The conscientious Christian will approach that decision with caution and skepticism: Is this divorce really necessary? The effect of the divorce on children of the marriage must be taken into serious consideration. Adequate financial provisions need to be made and carried out. Guidance from experienced and thoughtful counselors should be sought.

The final decision for a divorce can be made only by the persons involved. No amount of advice can substitute for the risk of personal choice. But once that choice is made, it is incumbent on the whole Christian community to show the divorced persons the love and care and support that will enable them to persevere through their crisis and begin to rebuild their lives. There is no room for moralistic judgment upon the brother or sister who has made that painful choice.

REMARRIAGE

While the church now finds it possible to sanction the remarriage of divorced persons, it is still advisable to undertake a second marriage only with considerable forethought. Second marriages suffer a high rate of failure. Once one has resorted to divorce as a strategy for dealing with a marital problem, it becomes that much easier to take the same route a second time.

A more subtle issue in second marriages is the persistence of unresolved conflicts left over from the first. Quite often those conflicts get projected into the second marriage without the partners even being aware of the fact. For this reason it is advisable for such couples to seek counseling from a pastor or marriage counselor.

The counseling process can help the couple to identify and work through unsettled issues arising from the experience of the former marriage and subsequent divorce. The new marriage can then start off on the soundest possible footing, thereby sparing the couple from potential disaster in the years to come.

PREPARATION FOR MARRIAGE

Couples contemplating a second marriage are not the only ones who need premarital counseling. Given the precarious character of marriage in today's society, careful and competent premarital instruction is a key to building any healthy and successful marriage relationship.

In the past, couples would often consult the clergy only to set their wedding date and to arrange the service. By that time, it is usually too late to do much serious preparation. Robert Capon has described his own experience in offering premarital instruction under such circumstances: ". . . being in the same room is about as close as we ever get to each other. I talk *marriage*; they think *wedding*."[5]

Because they have become painfully aware of the many hazards facing newly married couples, many clergy have developed thoughtful and thorough programs for marriage preparation. Usually these last for several sessions, are participatory rather than didactic in character, and seek to convey the church's teaching about marriage. At the same time, they help the couple to examine their own attitudes toward such things as money, sex, work, children, their own families, and the ways they handle conflict. They suggest the importance of seeking help when trouble comes; they acquaint the couple with the resources available to them.

Every priest who officiates at a marriage should provide such preparation for the couple, or at least should refer them to someone else who can do it. Some couples may resist the process, but most young people seem grateful for whatever help they can get in looking at the problems and possibilities that lie before them. A morally responsible church will do whatever it can to make that help available.

Family Life

Sociologists tell us that the family has undergone major changes in the period of industrialization and urbanization. In a rural agricultural society, the family was an economic unit. Children were assets because they helped with the work and they supported the parents when the latter became too old to contribute.

In contemporary society, however, the family no longer functions economically. It has become, rather, an emotional support group. The extended family of three or more generations, with its proliferation of uncles, aunts, and cousins has largely been replaced by the nuclear family consisting only of parents and their children, for that is the unit that moves most easily in our highly mobile society.

At the same time, the social context puts enormous pressure on the family, robbing it of the power and legitimacy it once had. Parents are no longer authority figures, regulating the information that tells the child what is real and what is not, what is true and false, good and evil. School teachers, newspapers and magazines, and, of course, the ubiquitous radio and television, all offer their competing views of reality, their value systems, their pronouncements about what is believable, what is important, what is in style. In such a setting the work of parenting becomes more difficult than ever, not because there are no guidelines, but because there are too many and they all conflict with one another.

RAISING CHILDREN

We cannot even claim to have a single "Christian model" for family life; a number of competing strategies for family living are available to us. Our society, for example, maintains an ongoing debate over how to raise children. In simplified terms, we could refer to "strict" and "permissive" child-rearing patterns.

The strict family will govern children by giving them clear and comprehensible rules for their behavior and will enforce those rules by appropriate punishment when violated. They will emphasize discipline and respect for authority on the ground that well-governed children will be better able to govern themselves upon reaching adulthood.

The difficulty in that approach is that children may conform in their outward behavior without ever giving inner assent to the rules. In that case, they are likely to resort to evasion, deception, and in extreme cases, outright rebellion. Even if they are well behaved, such children may grow up to be loveless and self-righteous.

A permissive family will offer their children more opportunity to exercise self-government. Children may be permitted to make their own choices rather early in life, even in important matters. Behavior may be indicated only in general terms and the child may be allowed to enforce those standards with only casual monitoring from the parents.

The value of this approach is that it teaches children to exercise freedom responsibly, learning the lessons of initiative and self-reliance. The hazard is that they may be bewildered and demoralized by having to face choices they are not equipped to make. Furthermore, the lack of guidance by parents may be compensated by the readiness of peers, trendsetters, advertisers, and other less savory forces in the society which seem all too eager to tell undecided people how they ought to behave.

Both these ways of raising children have their advantages and disadvantages. Moreover, the approach that is admirably suited to one child may be entirely inappropriate for another, even within the same family. A Christian perspective cannot guarantee the right choice of approach, but it can indicate the values to be pursued in either. Rules, for example, should always be clear and reasonable, admitting of exceptions when appropriate. Children should be helped to understand why an action is considered to be right or wrong, so that they learn to distinguish principles from the rules intended to embody them.

Every child should have opportunities to exercise freedom of choice in order to learn how to be responsible—and to live with the consequences of that choice. Parents are the best judges of what freedom can safely be allowed. They need to be conscientious without smothering the child with too much attention. Somehow parents have to find their path between the extremes of indifference and overanxiousness. Perhaps the most important thing that parents can do for their children is to share the values which they themselves live by.

The extraordinary diversity of our society puts a severe strain on the process of raising children. Different kinds of families have different values, different standards of behavior, and different expectations of their children. The least demanding standards tend to prevail as children quickly learn to complain: "Everybody else is allowed to do it. Why can't I?"

Parents recognize that, if their own values are to be affirmed and their standards upheld, they need help. The parish community can provide some of this support by creating opportunities for anxious or bewildered parents to come together to confer with one another and to enjoy the benefit of each other's experience. Groups of parents may even band together to develop common behavioral standards for their children. In the absence of the extended family, the parish church may be the only supportive community available to conscientious parents.

Still no one is perfect, not even parents. There is no guarantee that children will turn out the way their parents hope for them to be, no matter how well the parents perform their functions. The children may repudiate the highest values of their parents. In the finest Christian homes, children may stop going to church, lose their faith in God, live in ways their parents cannot condone.

It may be helpful for parents to realize that they cannot control the way their children will turn out, no matter what they do or fail to do. They are not necessarily to blame when things go wrong. Children are responsible human beings just as their parents are. Parenthood is a limited liability enterprise.

The British psychoanalyst Donald W. Winnicott coined a

term, "the good-enough mother" to describe the parent who gives her child enough room to engage in the fanciful kind of play that expands the imagination. That term is a perceptive one; it helps us to see that parents do not have to be perfect. They have only to be adequate to the task of training and nurturing the young. The parent anxious to achieve perfection will always wonder, "Did I do enough? Did I do too much?" It is pointless to agonize. Most parents will be "good enough" to raise reasonably adequate children.

That may be hard to believe at a time when children are going through what has become almost a cliche: teen-age rebellion, a process that may last for twenty years or more. Often what looks like rebellion is merely part of a movement toward what Kohlberg calls the postconventional stage of moral development.[6] Young people coming into adulthood need to assert themselves, often over against those who are closest and dearest to them, as a way of establishing their own identity. If all goes well, the child will ultimately come to accept the parents with all their faults and limitations, thereby opening the way to a new relationship of parent to child on an adult-to-adult basis. That new sharing of love, affection, and mutual respect may be the finest flower of modern parenthood.

GROWING OLD

The chief drawback of the nuclear family is that it has no place in it for old people. Most children in America grow up with very little regular contact with older people. Grandparents often live at some distance, so that children see little of them. Thus they miss the chance to see their own parents in the role of sons and daughters. They fail to see that what they may perceive as a unique generation gap is a persistent phenomenon in human history. They lack contact with family history, traditions, customs, rituals, and myths. Many adults likewise lose contact with their parents in middle age, thus losing valuable opportunities to work through unresolved issues in their relationship.

Foreigners coming to this country are frequently shocked

by our treatment of the elderly. They find it incomprehensible that we do not take primary responsibility for the care of aged parents. While their attitude is helpful in confronting us with an ethical issue we tend to disregard, they sometimes fail to understand that many older people prefer things the way they are. Older Americans are just as individualistic as the young. They value their autonomy. So long as it is economically feasible, most of them would prefer to remain on their own, rather than live in their children's homes. They do not want to be dependent, or to intrude on their children's privacy.

How can we best keep the biblical commandment to honor our fathers and mothers? That commandment was addressed not to children but to adults. What kind of honor do parents want and need?

At the very least, children should assume responsibility for the physical well-being of their parents. If retirement pensions are inadequate, if medical costs threaten, if older people require physical care, children ought to do what they can to see that their parents are relieved from care and worry. Beyond that, they need to keep in touch and not shut their parents out of their lives, for their own sake as well as for the parents' sake. Children need to know their older relatives, to the extent that communication is possible.

Where such contact is prevented by absence or death of the parents, children need other ways to relate to older people. Contact with the elderly in their own community offers a useful alternative to contact with unavailable grandparents. Children can learn to love and respect older people who live nearby, rather than ruling the aged out of our lives, as has happened too often in the past. Personal contact with people of all ages can help children to enlarge their understanding of what it means to be human, which was one of the valuable by-products of the extended family of a previous era.

THE SINGLE LIFE

No discussion of marriage and family life would be adequate without a positive word about the single life as well.

For our affirmation of genuine values is too often accompanied by an attitude of contempt, or at least indifference, to competing values. There is evidence that we have oversold marriage in our society. Since it is a Good Thing, we have acted as though everybody ought to be married. We try to match up our single friends. We treat marriage as a cure for personal shortcomings. We treat single people as though they suffered from some moral defect and we often exclude them from our company.

We live at a time, however, when there is no longer any compelling reason why everyone should be married. We certainly do not need the help of every adult to sustain the population. And when we consider the difficulties inherent in contemporary marriage, we are forced to conclude that many otherwise adequate and attractive adults may simply not be cut out for the married life. Thus we ought to accept and affirm the decision to remain single, just as we affirm the married state.

There are signs that we are beginning to make this shift. Single people are more generally accepted today than they were a generation ago. Still many married people leave their single friends out of their social lives. And churches which emphasize a family orientation often act as though single people did not exist, except perhaps for a special "young adult" group, which often serves as an informal dating bureau.

The Christian community, because it affirms and exalts the married state, has a peculiar obligation to affirm the legitimacy of staying unmarried. Churches need to open themselves up to greater participation by single people, in interaction with the married, so as not to treat singleness as a form of social disease.

Marriage and the Future

Our society is feeling a considerable degree of anxiety about the status of marriage and family life—and with good reason. A rising divorce rate, increasing evidence of troubled marriages, a variety of live-together arrangements that seem to indicate a repudiation of marriage by the young—not to mention such phenomena as swinging, open marriages, communal living, group marriages, free sex—all of these things support the view that marriage as we have known it is in trouble. Do marriage and the family have a future? What kind of future do they have?

Despite all the evidence to the contrary, we need not fear that either marriage or the family will disappear. These are the basic institutions of any society. They have proved tough and viable over many centuries. They may undergo considerable stress and significant changes, but we are too committed to them to let them die.

The stresses that we see in marriage and family life today are signs of significant changes and pathologies in the larger society. At the same time they represent efforts of the family to cope with and adjust to those changes.

We are beginning to see, for example, the effects of other social institutions on marriage and family life. The most prosperous members of the middle class seem to be the most vulnerable to frequent relocation, an experience that rips the family out of its social context, separating its members from friends, neighbors, familiar sights and sounds, and from other caring persons such as teachers, leaders, guides. Such families, left to their own resources, often become overly dependent upon one another.

Countless families, both rich and poor, find themselves subject to the pressures of a work life that removes the commuting or traveling father from the family circle. An increasing number of two-income families find that they can provide the children with all that money can buy but cannot provide what money cannot buy—caring and available parents. Even churches that proclaim the importance of family life nevertheless develop separate programs for every age group, thus contributing to the fragmentation of family life.

Some families are beginning to understand the effect of these external forces upon their corporate life. Some are going so far as to take direct action to cope with those forces, even though the cost may be high in terms of professional success or individual self-fulfillment. Men increasingly reject moves, even those that involve promotion, when it appears that their family will suffer too much from the dislocation. It is encouraging to see the readiness of people to preserve the stability of their family life in view of the price they have to pay.

We have begun to realize, then, that marriage and family life are not static conditions. "So they were married and lived happily ever after" is not a realistic or even credible comment any longer. Marriage in our time is a voyage in faith, a pilgrimage, as theologian John Snow has called it.[7] Over the long haul, the landscape may change, the people themselves will change, the issues change as will the nature of the relationship. The one constant in marriage is the commitment of the partners to one another, their conviction that, with care, patience, and a willingness to forgive and be forgiven, it will be possible to sustain their common life and to grow in love, trust, and affection in the process.

Christians see something profoundly sacramental about marriage. Paul saw in it a symbol of that mystical union between Christ and his church, which is to say that the deepest relationship between man and woman is somehow like the relationship between God and his people. Thus that relationship is close to the center of the Christian life. Christian men and women are called to bring that metaphor to the level of everyday reality as they live together in the love and trust and faithfulness to which the metaphor points.

Part Three

MORAL ISSUES
IN THE SOCIAL ORDER

· 8 ·

Christian Faith
and Social Morality

Some people see Christianity as an otherworldly religion which has to do primarily with the individual. The Gospel is addressed to our inward spiritual condition, our relationship with God. Alfred North Whitehead summed up this view when he said, "Religion is what the individual does with his own solitariness."[1]

Yet it is clear that the biblical faith has to do with things of this world. To claim that God is the Lord of history is to declare that he cares about what happens in this world—all of it. Indeed as Archbishop William Temple once pointed out, it is a mistake to assume that God is concerned exclusively with religion.

Most Christians have no difficulty in seeing the implications of faith for our private lives. We know that we are called to love God and to love our neighbors as ourselves. But we are tempted to limit that love to the neighbor who is close by, who is personally known to us. We can see moral issues in individual terms in such matters as family life, drug abuse, sex, truth-telling, but we tend to view the world outside the immediate and personal as being "secular." Behavior in those realms is governed by abstractions: the laws of economics, the realities of politics, or human nature. When Christians call for justice and humanity in the market place or in law enforcement, they are often regarded as naïve meddlers, out of place in the "real world."

Our religious tradition bears witness to another way of thinking. The prophets of Israel, for example, were just as vigorous in their denunciation of economic evils as they were in condemning idolatry. They denounced land-grabbing, unjust weights and measures, bribe-taking, and even the alliances of the king with foreign nations. Jesus observed how hard it is for the rich to enter into the kingdom. The Book of Revelation calls the Roman Empire the whore of Babylon. The medieval church taught doctrines of the just war, the just price, and the evils of usury.

The Christian cannot, therefore, suspend ethical judgment when entering the social world. Our behavior as citizens, workers, consumers, professionals, is still a part of our total Christian life for which we are accountable to God.

Individual and Social Morality

If the dilemmas of personal moral choice are complex and bewildering, those in the realm of social ethics are infinitely more so. In our personal dealings, human sinfulness makes itself felt in that we inevitably favor our own case. In social dealings, the same factor is present in a more extreme form. We inevitably see the world from the limited and distorted perspective of our own class, race, religious community, or age group.

Even those who are genuinely committed to justice and benevolence can see more easily the problems created for people like themselves by social policies designed for the benefit of others. Landlords who own real estate in urban areas can make a persuasive case for the absurdity of rent-control laws on the ground that they discourage upkeep and maintenance and drive investors out of the rental market. When discussing what constitutes an adequate profit in real-estate ventures, tenants will understandably have a different scale of values than landlords, even though each party may honestly be trying to sympathize with the plight of the other.

Beyond the built-in prejudice of every social group, there is a certain moral ambiguity in every group loyalty. As individuals, we can frequently subordinate our own self-interest for the benefit of those we love. A father, for example, may be quite unselfish in providing for his family, even if it means sacrificing his own opportunities for self-gratification. But his very unselfishness may lead him to acts of injustice against other families. A business manager may do things on behalf of the company that he would never condone if he were acting on his own behalf. This moral dilemma is captured in an aphorism attributed to the Italian statesman Camille Cavour: "If we were to do for ourselves what we do for our country, what rascals we would be."

In administering funds for a charitable institution, trustees may resist proposals that they should invest in ghetto enterprises, or that they should withdraw investments from companies doing business in South Africa. Their reasoning might take the form expressed by Hugh Cecil: "No one has a right to be unselfish with other people's interests."[2]

The moral dilemma in this instance is a conflict between two legitimate obligations. There is an obligation of trustees to exercise prudence in the management of funds committed to their care. There is also a peculiar obligation of charitable organizations to act in the larger public interest. They need to preserve their funds in order to survive, but they cannot exclude consideration of other social values.

In making their decisions, the trustees will have to balance these several obligations, in the context of the total mission of the institution. The point of the example is that it is more difficult to counsel the sacrifice of one's interest when that interest takes the form of an obligation to other people.

SOCIAL ISSUES AND MORAL CHOICE

Once upon a time there was a town that suffered from the constant presence of noxious fumes. The air smelled bad. It was sometimes hard to breathe. A light film of dirt covered everything in the town. Outsiders made jokes about it. Townspeople were embarrassed by it. Something had to be done.

There was no dispute about the source of the fumes. They came from the smokestack of a local manufacturing plant, the town's major employer. A physician claimed that the fumes were contributing to heart and lung diseases in the town. Activists planned a drive for an antipollution ordinance.

The plant manager denied the doctor's claim of a health hazard. "Sure the stuff smells bad," he acknowledged, "but there is no proof that any disease has ever been caused by the plant fumes. That ordinance will force us to close the plant. If that happens, a lot of jobs will be lost and the town will suffer. I wouldn't want that to happen. After all, I live here too."

The plant workers' union opposed the ordinance out of a concern over losing their jobs. But the activists denied that the ordinance would force the plant to close. Technology— stack scrubbers and filters—would enable the plant to eliminate most of the pollutant. Not so, countered the plant's engineers. Such sophisticated technology is too expensive for such a small plant. Its use would raise the cost of production so high that the plant would not be able to compete.

The townspeople were divided in their opinion. Whose side should the Christians be on? Significant moral issues were involved. How would the Christian reach a decision in this matter?

A conscientious Christian would ask certain questions in arriving at a decision. What are the facts? What are the moral issues? What are the choices? What are the goods and evils involved in those choices? Only after dealing with those questions would one be in a position to make an informed, conscientious decision. It won't be easy.

First, what are the facts? The only thing we can say for sure is that the facts are in dispute. Everyone agrees that the fumes are unpleasant, but are they dangerous? The physician says yes; the plant manager says no. Each has a vested interest in his position, so which one do you trust?

You might know that the physician is unusually wise and careful in his judgments, the plant manager a wily and crafty operator. Or perhaps you know the plant manager personally and find him concerned and humane but powerless in this situation. The physician may be an excitable worry wart or a publicity hound with a grudge against the factory.

Likewise, the claims for filter technology may be exaggerated, or the engineers may be lying to cover up for the company. Who knows? To make a decision you have to make up your mind about the facts. But which facts? Whose facts? Whom can you trust? What is the case?

What is at stake? The esthetic quality of life in that town, not to mention its self-respect as a community. The health of the people. The future of the plant. The economic future of the town. The welfare of hundreds of employees. The survival of the businesses (and the churches) that depend upon their support. Any one of these values may be paramount for a particular person.

What are the choices? Clean up the stacks? Close the plant? Or continue to tolerate the fumes? Which choice should a conscientious Christian make?

The only honest thing to say is that a conscientious Christian might conceivably opt for any of the suggested alternatives. Of course the clean-up would be preferable, but one might judge it to be impracticable on either technical or economic grounds. That person may be persuaded that, in view of the health hazard, the plant should be closed. Anyone who makes that choice should accept some responsibility for the loss of someone else's job and the consequent blow to the economy.

Another may conclude that the health hazard has been exaggerated and that the town can well afford to put up with the smell and the dirt in order to secure its economic future. Such a person should assume some responsibility for assuring that the worst effects of the fumes can be alleviated.

Which choice is the right one? From our perspective outside the situation, we cannot say. The rightness depends upon which facts are ultimately true, something that we can only judge for ourselves. We can never know for sure. Thus our choice can only be made in faith, on the basis of the best information we have available. Any of these choices might be a legitimate expression of genuine Christian concern for justice and the love of one's neighbor. The same choice might be made out of arrogance and insensitivity to the concerns of others.

I use this illustration—an unusual but not unheard-of situation—to demonstrate the difficulty in making responsible decisions about social issues. So much depends upon the particular facts of the case—or rather, upon our reading of those facts. Issues are controversial precisely because the facts themselves are usually in dispute.

To these facts we bring our principles: our concern for love and justice, for social harmony and the common good. And yet those principles are themselves in conflict: physical well-being versus economic welfare. Greater and lesser goods and evils have to be weighed.

Each choice involves some moral ambiguity. By doing good, we also do evil. Can we be sure that the good will outweigh the evil? The hidden costs of our choices may not show up for years, and yet the choice has to be made now.

In such complex situations, rules are of little use. Each situation is unique and needs to be understood in its own terms. Thus the approach of situation ethics seems most appropriate here. We come into the situation armed with our principles and presuppositions, but we need to get the facts first.

And our reading of those facts may differ from others who share our convictions. That is why Christians so often find themselves on opposite sides in matters of social policy. Christians, therefore, need to acknowledge and respect the integrity of those who come out on the other side of the issue. There is a saying: "You can't slice baloney so thin that it doesn't have two sides." The same can be said of moral choices in the social world.

We have to make choices. The facts may not all be in. We may not be sure whose version is true. There may be values on both sides of the question. Our friends may give us conflicting advice. Yet we have to choose. So we make our choice in fear and trembling, offering it up to the Lord with all its imperfections, asking his forgiveness for its inadequacies, respecting the integrity of those who conscientiously differ from us, keeping open to a possible revision if new facts come before us.

Such decision-making is both humble and responsible. It

may not always be right, but it will be faithful, and that is what Christian moral choice is all about.

MORAL PRESUMPTIONS: THE GOOD SOCIETY

Christianity does not imply a particular social, political, or economic system. It has lived, more or less comfortably, with many varieties of systems throughout its long history. For many centuries, monarchy was regarded as the most appropriate form of government for Christians. When the age of democracy dawned, the church was among the last of the major institutions to abandon the concept of kingship and to embrace the democratic idea.

But the shift was ultimately made and Christians today find that they can live out their faith in a democratic society. At various times and places, Christians have accepted capitalism, socialism, feudalism, aristocracy, mercantilism, industrialism, and countless other forms of political and social organization.

This is not to suggest that all systems are equal. Some seem more open than others to the possibility of maintaining Christian values. In order to make judgments about social structures and systems, we have to identify the moral presumptions that Christians would use to describe the good society.

Social justice would be a major Christian presumption. The social order should provide the necessities of life for all and should preserve its members from arbitrary or prejudicial treatment. The term "social order" itself suggests a presumption in favor of order, without which social life could not exist. Order enables people to live without fear, with the assurance that what is legitimate today will be so tomorrow, with the certainty of a stability that enables people to plan for the future.

Within that framework or order, Christians make a presumption about the value of freedom. A good society is one in which no one is oppressed or exploited by another. Each person and family is free to develop in their own way without penalty or coercion. At the same time, a reasonable degree of equality will insure that there will be no sharp disparity between the extremes of wealth and poverty, privilege and deprivation.

Finally, a good society will exhibit the quality of peace, both internal and external. It will be nonviolent; there will be no room for torture or terrorism. People will be treated humanely, both by the state and by other social institutions. As the prophet Micah sums it up, in the good society,

> . . . they shall beat their swords into plowshares,
> and their spears into pruning hooks;
> nation shall not lift up sword against nation,
> neither shall they learn war any more;
> but they shall sit, every man under his vine
> and under his fig tree
> and none shall make them afraid (4:3–4).

Church and Social Order

How can the Christian community help to bring about the kind of society which we believe would most closely approximate what God would want for his children? How should the church relate to its society? These questions are both complex and controversial. To put them into perspective, let us look at the way our views of Christianity and the social order were developed in history.

BIBLE AND EARLY CHURCH

If you look at the Bible with these questions in mind, you are struck by the difference between the Old Testament and the New. The Old Testament prophets were constantly telling the king, the rich, the powerful what they should or should not do. Their proclamations were addressed to the nation at large.

The New Testament, by contrast, has little to say about such matters. Kings and powerful people figure only peripherally in the New Testament. The faithful are called to a kingdom not of this world. Ethical injunctions are addressed, not to the nation but to the community of faith. It is this fact which has led many to suppose that Christianity is concerned only with the spiritual welfare of the individual.

The difference lies in the historical setting. In Old Testament times, Israel was a nation with national responsibilities. Prophets were concerned with the making of public policy. The New Testament events took place in a subjugated land, occupied by an invader. The Gospel spread in an empire in which Christians existed on the margins of society and, in order to survive, had to keep what we would call a low profile. Besides, most early Christians expected that it would all soon come to an end in any case.

The attitude of withdrawal from social concern prevailed until, under the emperor Constantine, Christianity became the dominant religion of the empire. From that moment on, the church took major responsibility for reshaping the pagan Roman Empire into a Christian social order. The story of medieval history is the tale of that enterprise. The church helped to civilize the barbarians who poured into Roman territories from the north and east. It brought the light of the Gospel to Europe and much of Asia as well. It developed a network of institutions for the education of the young, the care of the sick, the advancement of learning, and the preservation of culture.

THE ANGLICAN SOCIAL STANCE

This background helps us to understand the Anglican perspective on church and society, including that of the Episcopal Church. For that perspective was shaped by the experience of the Church of England which, as an established church, continued to see itself as the nation at prayer and to assume responsibility for the moral formation of the whole society. At its best, this tradition makes the church the conscience of the nation. At its worst, it encourages a certain ecclesiastical imperialism which suggests that bishops have the right to tell secular officials how to do their job.

The situation of the church in America is quite different. Here the nation is officially secular and the church's public role is circumscribed. Not only is there no established

church, but there are so many churches that the church seldom speaks with an undivided voice. It is difficult for the
average Christian to be sure of what the church says on any
matter of common concern.

Even in this environment, however, the Episcopal Church
has maintained a lively interest in the concerns of the larger
society. Indeed, when the growth of industry and city life
began to change the face of America in the late nineteenth
century, it was the old established churches: Episcopal,
Congregational, and Unitarian, that initiated the response
that became known as the Social Gospel Movement. In essence, that movement proclaimed that the Gospel of Christ
has implications, not only for our personal lives but for the
shaping of the whole society.

Today most Christian churches would agree with that insight, but not all would agree as to what are the implications
of the Gospel for our corporate life. There is no one model of
the good society. We may agree on some of its characteristics—such things as justice, freedom, and peace. But we
may differ sharply as to how those conditions can and should
be produced.

Thus some Christians favor government action as the major
vehicle for social change, while others favor voluntary efforts.
Christians may disagree about the amount of freedom that is
possible within the framework of a stable society. There is no
reason why Christians should be of one mind as to just how
the good society is achieved.

CHURCH STATEMENTS ON SOCIAL ISSUES

What is the "church" which speaks out on social and political issues? Most of us automatically think of official agencies.
In the Episcopal Church, we think of the General Convention
or of diocesan conventions. We think of clergy preaching
from the pulpit or bishops making statements to the press.

There is considerable disagreement about what the church
in these settings ought to be saying, or whether these agencies have any right to speak at all on matters outside the

spiritual realm. Their statements do not always reflect the views of most church members. They do not carry much weight with public officials. What purpose do they serve?

The major purpose of such statements is to inform and educate the church at large. At its best, a resolution of General Convention will represent serious and disciplined reflection by concerned and theologically informed church members on a matter of some importance. It should take into consideration the perspectives of people who see the issue in different ways. It should respect the consciences of those Christians who cannot accept its conclusions. And it should offer a basis for church members to come to their own conclusions about the matter.

CHURCH SOCIAL PROGRAMS

The church's concern for society goes beyond resolutions and rhetoric to the point of mounting programs and projects to act out that concern. In former times the church founded hospitals, schools, universities, and homes for the orphans, the elderly, and the poor. In more recent years, social action has increasingly brought the church into collaboration with government and private funding agencies which provide much of the financial support for church-sponsored social service projects. Head Start, hot lunch programs for senior citizens, social work agencies for the poor are often supported by grants from local or federal government, as well as from United Fund and other private organizations.

Some dioceses and even a few parishes have built housing for low-income people, especially the elderly poor. These projects are usually funded with federal money, though the church agency may provide seed money, preliminary studies, land, and continuing supervision of the project. The housing, as required by federal law, is open to all comers.

Such projects do not conform to a rigid doctrine of church-state separation, though it is hard to fault such collaboration when government does not interfere with the mission of the church and when the church, in turn, does not seek favored treatment from government. Some people wonder why the church should become involved in such secular business as housing at all.

That involvement can be justified if it is a conscientious response to the Lord's demand to love our neighbors as ourselves. It certainly requires the church to put its money where its mouth is, to act out what it calls others to do. Of course this presumes that the church is investing both time and money in the project, that it is not merely taking credit for an accomplishment when the government is taking all of the risk and paying all of the bills.

If the church is to engage in such enterprises, it should be able to insure a high level of performance. Church projects are too often sloppily run, as though the church's good intentions were enough. Church-run projects should be just as competently managed as those of any professional developer. If this is done, the church will experience the same moral dilemmas and make many of the same morally ambiguous decisions as those made by any secular dealer in real estate.

Perhaps it is good discipline for every reformer to have to meet a payroll, just like everyone else. Churches that have engaged in such projects have already learned that the problems of zoning, architectural design, unanticipated costs, and an unpredictable market all combine to make the work of the church agency just as complicated, frustrating, and hazardous as any secular business.

Beyond its commitment to competence, the church should be able to contribute something extra to its own social projects. It should exhibit a high level of human care and concern. Certainly those qualities can be found in nonchurch agencies, but anyone who has dealt with hospitals, schools, or social work agencies in recent years would concede that they are in short supply.

If a church is to engage in social action projects, those enterprises should manifest the compassion that propels the church into such enterprises in the first place. Those qualities should be evident to all who come into contact with the project: clients or tenants, employees, suppliers, and business associates as well.

The church, to be sure, is not primarily a social work agency. Its central purpose is the worship and service of its Lord, the proclamation of his Gospel. But because worship, service, and proclamation are at the center of its life, it can bring the qualities of that life into its social action as no other agency can. Thus, precisely because it is committed to the service of God and his children, the church can dare to be a social service agency—with a difference.

The Christian in the Social Order

Beyond the corporate involvement of the religious institution, the church is involved in the social order in the social action of every Christian. Christian behavior in marriage and family life contributes to the health of marriage and the family in the social order. A Christian working in a secular social agency may perform a more significant ministry than one working directly for the church.

This kind of activity is what we mean by lay ministry. In the normal routines of work, home, and even leisure, the Christian performs a ministry. It is important that we learn to identify this ministry so that we can bring it to a level of awareness. Only then can we learn to be more effective ministers of Christ where we are called to serve. For the ministry of the church is the ministry of the whole Christian people, not just that of the ordained, or of official ecclesiastical agencies.

This ministry can become more effective if church members come together regularly to talk frankly and freely about their life and work as ministry, to examine the presuppositions behind what they do, and to reflect theologically on the moral and ethical significance of their actions. All ministry needs this component of mutual support and accountability. We are doing lay ministry already. We need to learn how to do it more consistently, more self-consciously, and more effectively.

THE CHRISTIAN CONTRIBUTION
TO THE SOCIAL ORDER

As the foregoing discussion indicates, there are no easily formulated rules that Christians can follow in order to be sure they are doing the right thing in this vast and complicated area of social concern. Moreover it is important to remember that we Christians do not represent some neutral moral force that stands outside the thrust and counterthrust of social forces. We are all part of those forces as we participate in business, labor, industry, education, politics, and the market place.

But since we are Christians, we need to learn how our faith and our moral vision can be brought to bear in the social arena. It is sometimes enough to get the ethical issues identified and onto the agenda when decisions are to be made. At other times we may have special roles to play because of our work or professional activities. Some of us may take on particular issues and keep at them until we become sufficiently knowledgeable that we can make some special contribution. But in any case, we have a responsibility to get the facts straight, no small achievement when interested parties are only too glad to feed us their version of the facts.

The Christian moral vision operates at the intersection of the facts and our commitment. It is only by combining a good heart and a clear head that we will be able to serve the Lord in the social order.

· 9 ·

Contemporary Society in Moral Perspective

We have already seen how our social environment shapes our moral choices. We have seen further that society presents us with situations that call for moral choices. Beyond that, each society exhibits characteristics which themselves call for analysis and evaluation.

A given society, for example, may be isolated and ingrown, with a fear and hatred of strangers. A concern for the unity of the human family could lead Christians in that society to raise questions about the way strangers are treated. A society in which public order has broken down may raise moral questions about the right of individual self-defense and the need to develop ways of restoring order and stability.

Our own society has some characteristics which, while morally neutral in themselves, seem to offer both promise and peril. Let us look at six of these major qualities that shape our society and make it what it is. By seeing where the Christian interest lies in each of these areas, we can make our own judgments about what we would affirm, what we would accept, and what we would hope to change.

Urbanization

Central to our society is the fact that people gather together in increasingly large numbers. The term urbanization describes this phenomenon. It pertains, not only to the decaying core cities of the nation, but to the large metropolitan areas that encompass suburbs as well and are increasingly encroaching upon the countryside. There is no need to cite statistics to support this observation; we are all quite familiar with it. It is also obvious that urbanization produces significant changes in the way in which people relate to one another.

The urban environment makes each individual anonymous. Whenever you leave your own neighborhood and go out into the city streets, you find yourself among strangers. This experience leaves some people with a loss of their sense of identity. They get the feeling that they no longer have any assured existence. They feel lonely, frustrated, and sometimes angry as well.

This same anonymity tends to break down traditional social controls. Most of us are disposed to behave well when we are among people who know us. Even if we are not morally sensitive, we want to stay out of trouble. Among strangers, this sense of personal accountability declines. People quickly realize that they can do pretty much as they please and no one will know or care.

Urbanized people thus tend to become aggressive and self-preoccupied. Many of them get involved in experimentation with drugs, sex, and even crime and violence because these things provide thrills without much chance that the cost will be paid.

Urban life throws us together, but at the same time it cuts us off from one another. It breaks down those civilizing forces that bind us together; it makes us fearful and resentful of one another. People deal with this fear by separating themselves into homogeneous groups: the rich live in one area, the poor in another. White people live apart from black people, the young from the old. The fragmentation that results from this process challenges the moral vision of Christian people who believe in the solidarity of the human community.

Churches sometimes contribute to this fragmentation by the way in which they carry on their ministry. Our congregations are based primarily on our place of residence. Since our residential neighborhoods consist mostly of people who are similar in age, race, and income status, church life does little to bridge the chasms of metropolitan life.

Theologian Gibson Winter has suggested that the metropolitan community itself may be God's gift to us, as the instrument for bringing together the rich variety of the human family.[1] If Christian people are to contribute to this vision, they will have to find ways to swim against the tide of urban isolationism. To do so will affect their choice of residence, schools, friends, and even churches.

Christians in positions of power and influence can look at policy choices in the light of how real estate development or city planning can help to bring people together. They will try to discover what kinds of residential patterns will restore the vitality of neighborhood life so that people can better care for each other. Urban life can be urbane and civilized if we lavish care on those forces which humanize and personalize the urban landscape. Christians who believe in the unity of the human family have a natural investment in seeing that these forces are nurtured.

Diversity

The city is a center of variety and multiplicity where people of all ages, races, classes, and nations gather. The same could be said for this nation as a whole, for we have the most diverse population of any country on earth. America incorporates an amazing variety of races, religions, and national stocks, a bewildering assortment of ideals, philosophies, life styles, dress, food, and entertainment. Our greatest challenge as a nation has always been to discover how to "fashion into one united people the multitudes brought hither out of many kindreds and tongues," as the Prayer Book puts it.

THE BLACK EXPERIENCE IN AMERICA

The experience of Black Americans has been the most dramatic test of our capacity to achieve unity in diversity. Even after the abolition of slavery, black people have endured more than a century of oppression, segregation, discrimination, and prejudice. Even a generation after the Supreme Court decisions outlawing segregation, after a costly and lengthy struggle for civil rights laws, there is still much resistance to programs designed to achieve racial balance in schools and employment. Black families still lag well behind whites in levels of education, employment, and income. Even worse, these gaps do not appear to be closing. Unemployment among young black men is the highest in the country.

Despite efforts to establish in fact the equality we accept in theory, America is still a racist society. That is to say, skin color still determines how one is permitted to relate to the society, whether opportunities are available or not.

The drive to achieve a truly color-blind society has not succeeded. That, however, may be beside the point. Racial integration itself was merely the means to an end, the end being equality of opportunity and freedom of choice for all. Black people have fought for the right to live wherever they choose, the right to enjoy public accommodations, the right to schooling and employment. At one time these goals seemed to require that black people be entirely assimilated into white American society.

Many black leaders, however, came to see integration as a mixed blessing. It might be accompanied by the loss of significant cultural values and a weakening of those institutions that have enabled the black community to survive: the black church, the black college, black business and social groups, the black political power base.

This was the concern behind the frequent calls for "black power" that emanated from the corps of black militants. These leaders argued that black people would be best served by the affirmation of their own dignity and the preservation of their own institutions, culture, and heritage. Some called for total separation from white society, an unrealistic goal in this age of interdependence, but most black leaders have been willing to settle for preserving the uniqueness of black culture.

OTHER ETHNIC GROUPS

The wisdom of this attitude is attested to by a number of other American ethnic groups which have espoused similar views and slogans: Red Power, Green Power, Italian Power, etc. All bear witness to the need for various kinds of Americans to affirm their own unique cultural heritage, their traditional values, and their sense of peoplehood.

This point of view has become so widespread that we are learning to see American society in a new way. The traditional image of America as "the melting pot" is being abandoned in favor of the image of "the salad bowl" in which separate ingredients exist side by side, contributing to the flavor of the dish without suffering any loss of identity. A society that accepts this image of itself will be open to all without forcing any person or group to give up their inherited way of life in order to become a legitimate member of the community.

Yet group consciousness and group loyalty can subvert the unity of the whole body. The experience of other nations indicates that group rivalry can be a divisive force, leading to civil unrest and even civil war. It is difficult for a society to affirm unity and diversity at the same time, and yet our national motto, *e pluribus unum*, suggests that this is exactly what we mean to do.

Christians value diversity because it represents the richness of God's gifts to his people. How can we evaluate the way in which diversity is handled in our society? The status of black Americans provides the best test, for a black skin cannot, ultimately, be assimilated. If black Americans can find equal opportunity and acceptance while retaining the uniqueness of black culture, then the society will have passed the test. Until that day arrives, the whole society stands under judgment.

The church has a unique opportunity to show the rest of our society how to develop a united community out of a variety of peoples. The Episcopal Church, for example, includes a significant number of Black, Hispanic, American Indian, and Oriental members, but has not yet learned how to give equal place to all in the total life of the church. Despite its claims to catholicity, this church is still predominantly Anglo-Saxon in its orientation and will continue to be so until it has brought its various racial and ethnic groups into the mainstream of its corporate life. Only then will the church exhibit that unity-in-diversity which will testify to our belief in the unity of the human family under God.

Mobility

Americans are the fastest moving people on the face of the earth. It has always been that way with us, in contrast with most people throughout human history, who have lived and died within a very small geographical space.

America was populated by people who left their homes and traveled thousands of miles to get here. And once here, they kept moving across the continent, and later from the farms into the growing cities. In recent years, the immigration from Europe and Africa has been augmented by people from Latin America and Asia.

Movement has been social as well as geographical from the earliest days when the children of English yeomen produced a commercial aristocracy in New England and a plantation aristocracy in the South. Even today, children of poor immigrants are often able to obtain the education that will some day propel them into the ranks of the business and professional middle class.

Because of this experience, we tend to value mobility. We believe in "the career open to talent." "Stick in the mud" is a term of abuse. We change our jobs and our places of residence at an incredible rate. It is said that less than ten percent of the workers who participate in private pension plans ever stay on the job long enough (ten years) to qualify for benefits.

That is no great surprise in view of the fact that many workers know they are doing a good job only when they are offered a better one. Hence many people change jobs because it is the only affirmation they ever receive. If you have had no offers recently, the thinking goes, there must be something wrong with you. This attitude often produces a deep-seated restlessness which takes the joy out of work, even when the work itself is good and valuable.

Mobility is built into our consciousness in subtle ways. We have been taught that fulfillment is just over the horizon and we tend to take that literally. Thus many unhappy people believe that if they change their situation—get a new job or a new spouse, move to a new city—they will enjoy a fresh start and all will be well. But if the basic problem lies in the self, a move will only change its location. The problem moves right along with us.

We pay a personal cost for our mobility. As a people, we know how to adjust to new situations. We move with confidence, make friends easily, make quick adjustments. But since the possibility of leaving again is always in the back of our minds, we hesitate to form deep attachments. We find genuine intimacy difficult to achieve. We are left with tentative feelings about ourselves and others.

For many of us, mobility is not even a matter of personal choice. Our major institutions—business, government, academe, even the church—move people from place to place as a matter of policy. In subtle ways, movement makes the employee more dependent upon the institution and hence more loyal and docile.

These policies have disruptive effects on family life. A man may contemplate a move with real eagerness if it involves a promotion or an exciting new job, but his family may look at it quite differently. For the children it may mean the loss of friends, mentors, beloved places, a familiar way of life. For the wife it may mean a painful readjustment, or the abandonment of a budding career. Despite any improvement in family income and standard of living, the move may seriously jeopardize the quality of the family's life together.

Communities of highly mobile people suffer similar effects. In many towns populated by corporate executives or military personnel, the most capable people take the least interest in local affairs. Even local churches may suffer from a high turnover rate among parishioners.

Those engaged in policy-making need to be more conscious of the effects of such policies on the lives of other people. Human considerations need to find a more welcome place in personnel policies. Offices and factories should not be moved casually without concern for the uprooting of families that will be involved. Workers should not be penalized for refusing promotions that require a major move. Companies may even find it advantageous to have employees who are rooted in their community and who feel a loyalty to it.

Thoughtful Christians can recognize the positive moral values which mobility affords. Mobility keeps our future open. It keeps before us opportunities for change and renewal. It can be for all of us a source of hope and expectation.

But we need to understand the price it exacts in the loss of a sense of place, in the tearing up of our roots in a human community where we are known and cared for. Thus, movement, either physical or social, is a risky business, to be entered into only after a responsible weighing of the human benefit and cost.

Communication

A society that moves around so much needs to develop ways to keep in touch. That may be why we have witnessed the inauguration of a revolutionary era in the field of communication. Vast quantities of information are dispensed vividly and instantaneously through newspapers, magazines, billboards, radio, and, of course, the omnipresent television—not to mention the computers and copiers that have altered the conduct of business and institutional life.

INFORMATION OVERLOAD

The benefits of these technologies are obvious. We now know more about what is going on all over the world than anyone has ever known before. We have, to a great extent, achieved what Marshall McLuhan once called "the global village." We are as much a part of what happens on the other side of the world as of what goes on next door. Christians who believe in the unity of the whole human family can only rejoice in this fact.

This abundance of information has, however, some negative effects. When we are informed about everything that happens, we find ourselves inundated with more information than we can conscientiously absorb. We are left with the agonizing feeling that everything is going wrong and we can do nothing about it. We feel powerless and frustrated, an attitude that can lead us to be passive and unresponsive even in those areas where we are able to exercise some responsible choice.

ENTERTAINMENT AND REALITY

We have already discussed the morally questionable effects of television (and other) commercials that lead us to believe that the deepest concerns of our lives can be dealt with by buying the right product. We have also noted the passivity induced in the viewer by the entertainment that television makes so readily available.

The triviality of that entertainment is perhaps inevitable when there are so many hours to fill and so little creative talent available. Most shows are probably harmless if taken in small doses. The massive dosage of sex and violence that has been injected into much of television entertainment is more harmful. Parents, teachers, and church groups are only beginning to make their voices heard by the networks and forcing some change in program content.

A more subtle danger in television entertainment is the distorted view of the world that emerges on the screen. To young people, television offers answers to their basic questions of what the world is like, what ordinary men and women are like, what family life is like—or war, crime, politics, city life, country life, religion. Television's answers are a curious blend of fact and fantasy.

People who have been around for a while can discount much of what they see, separating out fantasy from fact. But to our children, television's version is the "really real." It provides the standard against which ordinary life is measured. Millions of young people have only a poor view of ordinary reality, which is not half as exciting as the television version.

For television reduces all of life to the level of show business. Even the evening news comes on as entertainment in which the bad news (the news itself) is played against the good news (the commercials). Short, snappy comments accompanied by vivid, though uninformative, film clips, keep the viewer occupied for the limits of a short attention span. Even the most significant issues, when treated in depth in hour-long specials, are processed into harmless packages of entertainment.

The entertainment motif has begun to invade the real world as politicians are packaged for glamor. Not "What does he stand for?" but "What image does he project?" is the question about the candidate. Public officials respond to opposition, not by altering their policies but by initiating campaigns to improve their image.

In entertainment, after a time every theme becomes boring, a fate that awaits public issues as well as situation comedies. Thus issues become fads: civil rights, urban decay, poverty, crime, drugs, hippies, the environmental crisis, the energy crisis, unemployment, inflation, world hunger. You can almost identify each issue by the year in which it was in style.

Once an issue gets identified, we have a batch of news stories, feature articles, TV specials to tell us all about it. Organizations emerge to mobilize public response to the issue, government programs are planned, foundations make grants.

Then at some magic moment, the issue becomes passé. Suddenly everyone is tired of hearing about it. We go on to the next fad/issue, usually without having done much about the last one. Has urban decay improved much since the riots of 1967? Has poverty disappeared?

The churches tend to follow these fads just the same as everyone else. Church groups have persisted in their response to the crisis of world hunger, to be sure, but our response has declined seriously since the year when it was *the* public issue.

The seriousness of Christian concern for any issue can be measured by the zeal with which we keep working on it after it has gone out of style. None of the major moral issues in our society will disappear after a television special or a new government program. The poor we will always have with us, which means that we are called to keep working to alleviate their poverty.

INFORMATION AND PRIVACY

The development of communication technology has produced new information systems that seriously threaten personal privacy. Computers make it possible to store up incredibly detailed information about millions of people. Through linkages among various information systems, it is possible for others to know more about us than we know about ourselves.

This knowledge gives others power over us, power that we may not even know about. If that observation seems faintly paranoid, just think of your last encounter with a computer that made a mistake in your billing. Such undetected errors have made it impossible for some individuals to obtain credit and have even accused others of crimes they did not commit.

The greatest perils of these information systems is not even known, because no one really knows the full extent of their capabilities. We have already seen that the most sophisticated systems can be invaded and manipulated. Our public policies regarding such systems are running far behind their capabilities.

For Christians the moral concern underlying our use of communication technology has to do with whether and to what extent it enhances the quality of human life. The cost to human freedom and personal privacy must be taken more seriously than it has to date. The society has no right to violate the integrity of persons, whether the means be physical or electronic.

Technology

The field of communication offers only one illustration of the way in which society is reshaped through the use of modern technology. Technology has made modern urbanization itself possible, through the creation of water and sewage systems, gas and electric power, lighting, the automobile, the refrigerated truck, the elevator, the telephone and an incredible number of other devices we have learned to take for granted. Without advanced technology, modern society as we know it simply could not exist.

Many people who recognize this fact have come to deify technology, seeing in it a savior that can deliver us from all our troubles. Is there a problem? Research will find an answer and the engineers will produce something that will solve it. Any money spent on technological innovation is regarded as well spent, for it is devoted to Progress, against which there is no argument.

Recently that attitude has begun to sour, as technology has been blamed for creating problems rather than being credited for solving them. We are coming to realize that problems are seldom solved, but rather that, in eliminating one set of conditions, we often create other conditions that we neither wanted nor expected. There is a trade-off in technology. You get something; you give something up. Sometimes the price seems too high to pay.

This skeptical attitude toward technology has grown into an antitechnological crusade. Reacting to the failure of technology as a god, some people have made it into a demon, the cause of all our woes. The simple life is once again extolled and people are urged to abandon the use of technology in favor of ways of living that were current a century ago.

Undoubtedly that attitude represents an overreaction. But if we cannot abandon the use of technology, perhaps we can reduce our dependence upon it. We can back off from our commitment to inordinately complex, expensive, and unreliable technology. We can develop criteria to guide public policy in the development and use of technology.

Social critic Paul Goodman once suggested that we should use technology sparingly, and then mainly to simplify. That rule would enable us to regard technology as neither savior nor demon, but rather as a useful servant who can be very helpful as long as he knows his place—a good servant, but a poor master.

For most people, decisions about technology come in small packages. Shall I buy a second car—or even a first one?

Should we think about moving away from a location where we are entirely dependent upon the automobile? Should I buy an air conditioner? Another radio? An electric can opener?

Those who hold responsible positions in business or other institutions are faced with more complex decisions. Should we move toward automation in order to produce a cheaper product, or will we create too many social problems by throwing people out of work? Do those expensive computers give us more information than we can productively use? While the trade-off is sometimes hard to compute, it is important that both the costs and the benefits be identified so that the decision about technology can be made in full realization of what is at stake.

This attitude must be applied to the development of public policy regarding technology. We have learned that the experts cannot always be trusted to tell us how to treat technology because they often have a stake in its development. We are told, for example, that nuclear power plants are safe because accidents are highly unlikely and, therefore, the hazards are minimal. But the advocates of nuclear power become tongue-tied when the subject of atomic waste is raised.

The fact is that the experts differ sharply over the safety of nuclear power, so that both proponents and opponents can produce their own experts. The decision about nuclear power development, therefore, is a political, not merely a technological, choice. It should be made only after full consideration of the possible human costs involved. The same can be said for any other policy regarding the development and use of technology. Ordinary citizens affected by those policies need to make their voices heard, along with those of the experts who have, until recently, tended to dominate the public discussion of technological choices.

Christians cannot pronounce technology either good or evil, for it is morally neutral in itself. The uses of technology, however, raise moral questions. It is our responsibility to see that significant questions get raised and answered. We cannot allow simple-minded notions of inevitable progress or unsubstantiated claims of enormous benefits to cloud our own judgment about the particular goods and ills that a particular technological choice may bring with it.

The Physical Environment

The chief hazard in our heavy use of technology is its effect on our physical environment, which is why concern for the environment has become a social and political issue. There was a time when we could take nature for granted. It was merely the backdrop for the drama of human progress. In our own country, both land and resources were so abundant as to seem inexhaustible. There seemed to be no reason why they should not be used extravagantly.

Today, as a result of population growth, technological change, industrialization and urbanization, we are beginning to perceive the limits of what the physical environment can tolerate in the way of human interference. Thus we are experiencing what, for the first time, can be called an environmental crisis.

ASPECTS OF THE CRISIS

One form of the crisis is the depletion of our stock of natural resources. We are using up minerals at a rapid and ever-increasing rate. When we speak of "the energy crisis," we really mean that there is only so much petroleum and natural gas in the ground. One day it will surely run out. In the meantime, it can only become more and more costly.

A second form of the crisis is the destruction of plant and animal life. The use of chemical pesticides has affected the food chain, threatening several species of predators. Drainage of swamps and marshland upsets the delicate ecological balance. Conversion of land to housing and highways destroys the habitat that supports many smaller mammals and birds. Overfishing and oil spills threaten sea and river life. These changes are going on all over the world to the extent that many species of animal life face extinction.

The contamination of our air and water supplies threatens every one of us because there is no place to flee from the consequences. Air quality in our major metropolitan areas reaches dangerously poor levels for extended periods. The economic cost of such pollution is incalculable. Most of our rivers have become unusable for fishing, swimming, or drinking. We spend immense amounts of money on water purification, while using our waterways as open sewers at the same time.

The chemical pollution of air and water is accompanied by the increase of chemical additives to the food we eat. One after another flavoring agent or preservative is found to cause cancer in laboratory animals, so that many researchers now believe that such factors are primarily responsible for the alarming rise in the rate of cancer in our population.

Many of these facts have been greeted by public demands that something be done, but little has been achieved. Air quality information is now included in many local weather reports with the result that, rather than generating concern, they have gotten us accustomed to pollution alerts. Reports of cancer-causing agents in our foods are greeted with public apathy: "Oh, another one? It looks like everything causes cancer, so why bother?"

CHRISTIAN INVOLVEMENT

For Christians the care of the physical environment is a significant moral issue. Many people outside the Christian community blame the Christian perspective for our present crisis. After all, God tells mankind to

> Be fruitful and multiply, and fill the earth and subdue it; and have dominion over . . . every living thing that moves upon the earth (Gen. 1:28).

That passage encourages an exploitative attitude toward nature, we are told, an attitude that has characterized the Christian era of world history. It is true, of course, that the central proclamation of the Old Testament is God's lordship over history, while his lordship over nature seems relegated to the background. But it is also true that we have downgraded the importance of nature by a very selective reading of the biblical texts.

The Bible does not deify nature as did the pagan cults of the ancient world. In the Bible, nature is merely a creature. But it is part of God's creation, as the creeds assert, and God saw that it was good. The psalms invite us to view nature with reverence, seeing in the natural order the loving and creative hand of God. Mankind, according to the Bible, has been given stewardship over the earth and is therefore responsible to God for its care and nurture.

That has always been true, but only recently has it become important. The reason for the change is that in the past nature had the advantage: it was so big and we were so small. Nature was the great adversary, the great challenge. The human race had to fight hard against nature in order to survive. Cold and heat, famine and flood, animals and insects, desert and wilderness, all threatened the human enterprise. Mankind had all it could do to hold its own against these powerful forces.

But today, through the use of technology, we have largely achieved the long dreamed of conquest of nature. Our dominance is so complete that the natural order itself is threatened by the aggressive technological civilization. The moral issue for the future will be how to keep nature alive and healthy, so that the human enterprise does not, by its very success, bring destruction down upon its head, fouling its own nest and making it uninhabitable.

Thus the care of the earth is now a major moral concern for all thoughtful and responsible people. Christians need to develop a "nature ethic" that will help us to clarify what is and what is not legitimate activity in the light of the environmental crisis.

These concerns have been derided by some as being a "middle-class trip" confined to those who are already affluent and comfortable. Such people, it is said, can afford to worry about snail darters, can demand that the woods and beaches be kept clean for their recreation. But, the argument runs, environmentalists can subvert economic progress. The cost of their interference will be paid by the poor who will be deprived of the jobs that only economic development can make available to them. The third world has plenty of clean air and water, along with poverty. Third world people would gladly trade for dirty air and prosperity.

Perhaps they would, but it is not entirely clear that economic development requires the despoiling of nature. What is clear is that the contamination of air and water—even the oceans—is reaching the point of irreversibility. Polluted water can destroy the fishing industry, as well as raise the price of water purification. Atomic wastes will remain radioactive for centuries.

These issues may be the most difficult and complex of all those we face as a people. Christians can claim no easy or certain answers, because each decision that affects the environment has its own built-in costs and benefits. What we do know is that we are called to responsible stewardship for God's creation.

In our capacity as consumers, as business managers, as policy makers, as legislators, it is incumbent upon us to take these environmental issues into consideration as we make our decisions. To do so may mean that it will cost more to make some products. Some lines of activity may have to be phased out. The price we pay for some goods may have to rise. But we can afford to pay the price if it means the preservation of our most priceless heritage: the created world itself.

SOCIAL STRUCTURE AND MORAL VISION

What we have been discussing in these pages are not moral issues in themselves, but rather phenomena which call for moral reflection and decision-making. They serve to illustrate the fact that the Christian moral vision extends beyond our private lives to encompass the very fabric of society itself. Christian responsibility calls for us constantly to expand our moral vision until all of life—and nature itself—is included in our concern to see God's reign of love and justice established upon the earth.

· 10 ·

Medicine and Health Care

I have chosen to devote an entire chapter to medical issues for two reasons. First, medical matters are very close to all of us. We are all subject to the ills of the flesh. We all face death and the deaths of those who are close to us. We all, therefore, have a strong interest in medical matters.

Second, the practice of medicine has undergone major changes in recent years. Medical research has brought to our doorstep issues that would have been inconceivable even one generation ago. The advance of medical technology has created situations in which someone must make a conscious decision about who is to live or to die.

Four Major Issues

Conscientious Christians have a stake in how these decisions are made. We need to understand how our moral vision affects those choices. Let us look, then, at four major issues: abortion, biomedical research, the delivery of health care, and the facing of death.

ABORTION

Abortion has surfaced as a major ethical controversy in recent years. We have begun to recognize that, when abortion was strictly illegal, some women turned to illegal practitioners who worked under unsanitary conditions and often lacked even rudimentary training, with a resulting toll of infection, disease, and even death. Now that the laws have become more permissive, the question has been forced upon us: is abortion ever morally permissible? If so, under what circumstances?

Christians are deeply divided on this issue. Many uphold the view that abortion is equivalent to murder. Others believe that abortion is a morally neutral medical procedure, to be decided upon by the pregnant woman in consultation with her physician and that any law or morality that seeks to influence that decision is illegitimate. Within nearly every Christian communion, some advocates can be found for each position and for many positions between those extremes.

The two views are incompatible because they begin at different points, each of which excludes the other. We need to look critically at the entire question from the perspective of our Christian moral presumptions, so that we may begin to develop a common mind on the matter.

Early Christians regarded abortion as morally wrong. By the sixteenth century, however, distinctions were made which would permit abortion in certain circumstances—to save the life of the mother, for example. Theologians distinguished between the formed versus the unformed fetus, a distinction based on Aristotelean theory which held that a rational soul developed in the fetus somewhere between forty and eighty days.

But while the rhetoric of popes and theologians equated abortion with murder, it was never treated quite that harshly in practice. Penalties for abortion were never as severe as were those for murder. This discrepancy suggests that, while logic dictated one response, the common-sense view of the matter was much different. The official view was adhered to in theory, while a less stringent view was applied in practice.

Roman Catholic treatment of the issue has focused almost exclusively on the status of the fetus. Modern science has repudiated the Aristotelean theory in favor of a developmental concept of fetal life. From the beginning the fetus has its own genetic endowment, different from that of either mother or father, yet it lacks those characteristics of consciousness and personality which make us fully human. Its nervous and circulatory systems develop during the gestation period until the fetus becomes viable, capable of surviving outside the womb.

While that information is important, it does not help us to decide just when the fetus ought to be endowed with those rights that pertain to the fully developed person. That determination cannot be made on the basis of mere physical data, but only from our moral and ethical perspective.

Roman Catholic thinkers have, on the whole, held to the view that, from the moment of conception, the fetus is to be regarded as fully human with full human rights. This view has led to a continuing condemnation of abortion under nearly every circumstance. Non-Catholic theology has had little to say about the matter, a fact which has led many non-Roman Catholics to accept the most extreme Roman Catholic view without much reflection on the matter.

In his very excellent study of abortion, Daniel Callahan has noted that the traditional Roman Catholic view has preempted the discussion of abortion because if the status of the fetus becomes the primary issue, then all other factors are ruled out of consideration.[1] But a decision about abortion is a complex human choice, not to be reduced to a single factor. The health of the mother, her psychological condition, her duty to her other children, the economic situation of the family—all of these factors can influence a conscientious choice regarding abortion.

How can these competing values be adjusted? The Bible itself offers little direct help, since abortion as a moral issue is not raised in the biblical literature. The commandment to do no murder may raise the question but does not settle it. The traditional Roman Catholic position, resting on narrow biological grounds and argued logically to a predetermined conclusion, is proving unsatisfactory even to many Roman Catholic theologians who are concerned to see abortion in the full context of its human significance. That consideration will include medical, psychological, and even economic aspects of the total situation.

Opponents of abortion tend to write off all considerations other than the human status of the fetus. The other matters are regarded as concessions to convenience and selfish interests. While these criticisms may sometimes apply, pastors who have counseled women seeking abortion can testify that in many cases their situation is truly desperate and their dilemma can hardly be described in terms of selfish interest. An overburdened mother of many children, with inadequate income, in delicate health, and under great personal stress may not be in immediate danger of losing her life, but the human quality of that life may indeed be in jeopardy.

Should abortion be available on demand then, as some propose? Is abortion a morally neutral medical procedure, not essentially different from having an appendix removed? Does a woman have an absolute right to control her own body?

Christians, as we have already seen, do not believe that we have absolute freedom over our own bodies, for as Paul quite appropriately reminds us, "You are not your own; you were bought with a price" (1 Cor. 6:19–20). We are stewards of our bodies and are accountable for how we make use of them. We have no absolute right to do whatever we wish with our bodies.

But it is true that only individual persons can take full responsibility for what is done to their own bodies. Thus the responsibility for making a decision about abortion must ultimately rest with the woman who is pregnant. She must make that decision in conformity to her own convictions and in response to her own perception of her situation.

The fact that a fetus has its own genetic endowment different from the mother's argues against the view that it is merely a piece of tissue, just as expendable as an appendix. Since the fetus has its own existence, even within the womb, it must be regarded as potential human life.

But potential human life is not the same as actual human life. For that reason, I believe it is legitimate to treat a fetus differently from the way we treat a fully developed human being. A fetus is not a baby. Abortion is not murder.

If we accept the developmental view of fetal life, we must recognize the difference between an early fetus and one that is viable. Some laws, recognizing this distinction, permit abortions only in the first three months of pregnancy. Great caution must be exercised in determining just when the fetus should acquire the protection of the law, but though such distinctions are difficult, they nevertheless have to be made.

The bias in the Christian moral vision is toward the preservation of life. The Christian moral presumption, therefore, is in favor of protecting fetal life. This does not mean that abortion is an illegitimate choice in every situation, but it does mean that it is a morally serious decision, one to be made only after all other possibilities have been proved inadequate or unfeasible.

The General Convention of 1976 considered this issue and produced a very thoughtful resolution that deserves to be cited in its entirety:

> *Whereas*, it is imperative for the Church as a Body of Christ to provide clear guidelines for human behavior which reflect both the love and judgment of God, now therefor be it
>
> *Resolved*, the House of Bishops concurring, that the following principles and guidelines reflect the mind of the Church meeting in this 65th General Convention:
>
> 1. That the beginning of new human life, because it is a gift of the power of God's love for his people, and thereby sacred, should not and must not be undertaken unadvisedly or lightly but in full accordance of the understanding for which this power to conceive and give birth is bestowed by God.
>
> 2. Such understanding includes the responsibility for Christians to limit the size of their families and to practice responsible birth control. Such means for moral limitations do not include abortions for convenience.
>
> 3. That the position of this Church, stated at the 62nd General Convention of the Church in Seattle in 1967 which declared support for the "termination of pregnancy" particularly in those cases where "the physical or mental health of the mother is threatened seriously, or where there is substantial reason to believe that the child would be born badly deformed in mind or body, or where the pregnancy has resulted from rape or incest" is reafffirmed. Termination of pregnancy for these reasons is permissible.
>
> 4. That in those cases where it is firmly and deeply believed by the person or persons concerned that pregnancy should be terminated for causes other than the above, members of this Church are urged to seek the advice and counsel of a Priest of this Church, and, where appropriate, Penance.

5. That whenever members of this Church are consulted with regard to proposed termination of pregnancy, they are to explore with the person or persons seeking advice and counsel other preferable courses of action.

6. That the Episcopal Church express its unequivocal opposition to any legislation on the part of the national or state governments which would abridge or deny the right of individuals to reach informed decisions in this matter and to act upon them.[2]

The question of public policy regarding abortion has been especially controversial because of the sharply differing views held by various religious and political groups. Callahan argues that the law should be very permissive, providing only that those who perform abortions be medically competent and that a woman seeking an abortion should have access to counseling that would help her to find alternatives where possible.

Such permissive laws will be offensive to those who believe that abortion is murder. But in a pluralistic society, when the community is genuinely divided over the moral status of particular acts, the law must be very reluctant to enforce one view against all the others. Legal toleration of acts we do not ourselves condone is necessary in those areas where our consciences conflict.

BIOMEDICAL RESEARCH

The amazing development of medical research and technology in our generation has confronted us with a complicated array of ethical issues never before faced by the human race. Artificial insemination, *in vitro* conception, organ transplants, have all proved feasible and may some day be commonplace.

In the field of genetic research, scientists have identified the defective genes responsible for a number of congenital defects and diseases. Some believe that it may be possible to repair defective genes so that the disease may be prevented, or at least mitigated.

It has been suggested that genetic manipulation may some day make it possible to produce desired physical characteristics, from choosing the sex of the unborn child to determining its size, hair color, or whatever other trait seems desirable to the prospective parent. Cloning—the creation of a new cell that possesses the exact genetic characteristics of the parent cell—has been proposed as feasible. The result would be something quite new: a person with the same genetic endowment as the parent.

Moral Presumptions

How are we to make responsible ethical decisions about such matters? Precedents are unavailable because the issues themselves are novel. They involve facts of enormous technical complexity, about which even the experts disagree. Are there principles that can help us to make up our minds about the responses we are called to make in these most perplexing areas?

Our Christian moral presumptions would include a fundamental concern for preserving and enhancing the quality of human life, a concern to preserve the integrity of the family and the care of children, a concern for healing the sick and relieving human suffering, and a long-range commitment to the welfare of the whole human family. At the same time, we would insist that people involved in making decisions in medical matters be given sufficient information to enable them to make free and responsible choices.

In the light of these presumptions, artificial insemination using sperm from the husband would seem to pose no major difficulties. Its value is in offering the possibility of having children to couples for whom the natural process of impregnation does not work effectively.

Artificial insemination by a donor is more complicated because it produces a child whose biological father is not the legal parent. Couples considering this procedure should give careful thought to the possible effects on the psychological health of the child and on the stability of the marriage itself.

Experimenters have already enjoyed success in their efforts to implant in a mother's womb an egg which was fertilized with her husband's sperm in a laboratory. Thus the baby conceived in a test tube, or its equivalent, is already a reality. The first of such children was born fully normal and free from birth defects.

That fact should not, however, blind us to the hazardous nature of the proceeding. In selecting one fertilized egg for implantation, the experimenter must discard other fertilized eggs which are then destroyed. Does that act constitute a multiple abortion? If so, is that a necessary and legitimate consequence of a morally defensible procedure? Does the procedure entail the likelihood of producing deformed children? Such questions may suggest the abandonment of the procedure on the basis of the medical dictum, "First of all, do no harm."

There is, to be sure, a positive value in enabling a couple to have children who might not otherwise be able to do so. Christians can only approve of the relief of human suffering. The attempt to develop ways to overcome impotency is itself a valid enterprise. But the means employed should be examined with caution before decisions are made in this area.

Genetic Research

Genetic research offers the promise that some congenital diseases can be treated by supplying the deficiency caused by the defective gene. The use of insulin to control diabetes is a case in point. Some researchers believe that it will some day be possible to manipulate the defective gene itself, thereby eliminating the defect before the disease develops. Others doubt that genes can be manipulated without the danger of terrible and unwanted consequences. Responsible Christians would be well-advised to look with caution upon these developments and not be too quick to accept the claims of their most enthusiastic proponents.

It is already possible to detect some major genetic defects in an unborn child. Genetic counselors can help parents to consider their response to the possibility that their expected child may be badly deformed. They may decide on an abortion if the risk of extreme deformity is high.

In these cases, genetic information may seem a mixed blessing. It enables the prospective parents to make a responsible and informed decision, but it also makes a decision mandatory where, without the information, the parents would just take whatever comes without exercising any choice at all. Thus they are given both the opportunity for and the burden of responsible moral choice.

Ethical Aspects of Public Policy

Christian moral presumptions make us wary of the indiscriminate acceptance of any and all forms of medical research in the name of the search for truth. While most research has for its purpose the elimination of suffering and disease, some scientists in the medical field, as in other fields, are inspired by an itch to know, which can be productive of as much harm as good.

The preoccupation of some scientists with elaborate experiments designed to create human beings through technological interventions needs to be questioned. The creation of living substances in the laboratory, attempts to bring a fetus to full term outside the womb, cloning, and other exotic procedures have little relevance to human health and well-being.

We are often told that these experiments will be carried on no matter whether we want them or not, but is that necessarily so? Medical research is carried on largely with grants from foundations and government agencies. The funds are committed because some people have been convinced that the research serves the public interest.

Decisions as to how those limited funds are to be used ought to be based on a sense of moral priorities. Studies designed to increase our knowledge of genetic defects are justified insofar as they help us to make better informed decisions about treatment. But in an age of overpopulation, it is difficult to justify the allocation of scarce resources to find new ways to make more human beings. The old way seems to be working only too well. When research proposals are evaluated, the moral question needs to be asked: "How will this project enhance the quality of human life?"

At the same time, patients and other subjects of medical research should be given enough information to enable them to make responsible and informed choices. Experimenters have been known to overplay the possible benefits of a new, untried procedure, while downplaying the possible side effects.

Parents of a stricken child, for example, are especially vulnerable to suggestions that anything is worth trying if there is the slightest chance that it will prove beneficial. Competent and sensitive counseling should always be available to persons in that situation so that their consent can be truly free and responsible.

Exercising Christian Responsibility

How can Christians exercise moral responsibility in such an extraordinarily complex field, so full of highly technical issues beyond the competence of the nonscientist even to understand?

Some Christians, of course, share in this competence as physicians, scholars, and policy makers. They can contribute to the formation of public policy by bringing their moral vision to bear on their professional concerns. While they may not always agree, they will at least share a common ethical perspective. Some universities and government agencies have already begun to include on research committees persons with specialized training in ethics, so that these concerns are introduced into discussions about research proposals and grant allocations.

Christians who are themselves engaged in medical research can incorporate their moral presumptions into their work. They can exercise restraint with respect to the kind of experimentation they will undertake; make sure of the informed consent of any experimental subjects; take care to avoid damage to, or careless treatment of, patients and subjects, living or unborn; make the enhancement of human life the ultimate purpose of their investigations.

Finally, even those of us who know little about these matters may, on occasion, be called upon to make judgments that will affect our own lives, the lives of those close to us, and even generations yet unborn. It may involve a donation for a transplant; a decision to abort a severely deformed fetus; a request to serve as a subject in a test of a new medicine or medical procedure.

Should that happen, these presumptions may help to guide our decision. More likely we will want to ask for help. Such help is now available in most sections of the country, as more and more ethical thinkers devote themselves to questions of medical research and practice. Through the use of both technical competence and loving concern, the bewildered may find resources that will enable them to make the fitting choice.

HEALTH CARE

Most of us will probably never be involved directly in the more esoteric aspects of medical research, but we all have significant relationships with the medical community, what politicians have begun to call "the health care delivery system." The thing we notice most about it is the cost. Hospitalization insurance has become a major family expenditure. Despite governmental assistance—Medicare and Medicaid—health care costs are prohibitive for the poor and the elderly.

Patients claim that physicians' incomes are too high, the highest by far of any professional group. Physicians complain about the exorbitant cost of malpractice insurance. Both complain about the deterioration of the traditional physician-patient relationship.

Rising health care costs have many causes. Labor costs in hospitals have risen sharply. Poor planning has resulted in an oversupply of hospital capacity. Hospitals have overinvested in highly expensive but rarely used equipment. Since a large share of the cost of health care is paid by third parties—insurance plans and government programs—there is little incentive to keep costs down.

Beyond questions of medical economics and technology lies a deeper spiritual issue. It has to do with the loss of faith that renders us vulnerable to the exploitation of our fear of suffering and death.

When our deepest convictions lead us to trust in God, who

supports us in life and death, we are empowered to face the risk of suffering and pain with courage and confidence. While our health is important—we are stewards of the bodies God has given us—yet the state of our health need not be an all-consuming passion.

For many people in the modern world, faith in God has been replaced by faith in something called medical science which, people believe, can or should cure any illness. When it fails to heal, then someone must have done something wrong. Some physicians themselves are motivated by this point of view, feeling a sense of personal failure and defeat whenever a patient dies while in their care.

Despite the use of X-rays and biochemistry and sophisticated technology, the practice of medicine is still something of an art. It still requires imagination, guess work, trial-and-error methods. Physicians still do not always understand just what they are doing. They are not always sure just what their medications will do for or to a particular patient. Medical practice is a risky business and no one can take the risk out of it entirely.

Because we have such high expectations of medical science, we tend to overuse physicians, hospitals, and medications. Some physicians maintain that most of the people they see in a normal day do not really need a physician. They suffer from aches and pains, from some temporary ailment that could best be treated by rest and nourishment. These "worried well" patients want assurance rather than treatment, but they take up as much of the physician's time as those who are seriously ill.

By the same token, much medicine is dispensed for psychological rather than physical reasons. Some patients do not seem to feel they have been taken seriously unless they emerge from the examining room with a prescription. Tranquilizers are dispensed by the ton, mostly to people not in deep distress. Millions of dollars are spent each year on cold medicines, although everyone knows that, at present, the common cold is incurable.

The reason behind this overuse of medical facilities is that many people are desperately afraid of suffering, aging, pain, disability, and, finally, death itself. Convinced that only medicine can save them, they will meet any expense to insure their health. Whatever hospitalization and medical care may cost, their response would be, "Well, if it can save my life, it's worth it." No wonder medical costs continue to rise!

This simple faith in the absolute power and wisdom of the medical profession has led many patients to adopt a totally passive attitude toward medical practitioners. "Father knows best" is replaced by "Doctor knows best." As in so many other areas of life, people tend to turn their most serious problems over to specialists, resigning themselves to complete helplessness in dealing with matters relating to their own health.

Some physicians encourage this dependency, adopting an authoritarian demeanor that intimidates the patient. The physician may tell the patient little about his ailment, or explain it in a confusing medical jargon that is incomprehensible to the lay person. The patient defers to the physician's judgment, doing as he is told, asking no questions. In hospital, the good patient is the one who is closest to being inert, making no complaints, being totally compliant, raising no questions or objections.

Those who place their deepest trust in the transcendent power of God will find it difficult to yield to this uncritical faith in medical science. What kind of response might the faithful Christian make to the dilemmas posed by sickness and disability?

First we would affirm the value of the healing arts as the gift of a loving God, to be used for our good. At the same time, we would recognize the limits of medicine. Physicians and other medical practitioners are fallible humans like ourselves. They depend on human skill and imagination. They can make mistakes. We have the major responsibility for decisions affecting our own health. We need to reject the dependent role of passive patient and learn to collaborate more actively in our own healing.

We can practice preventive medicine by providing for ourselves and our families proper nutrition, exercise, and rest—nature's best and most generally available health cures.

We should select a physician with some care. We want one who is competent, one who keeps up with developments in the field, one who uses medications judiciously, one who is willing to offer explanations of proposed remedies, including both benefits and risks.

In our dealings with health professionals, we need to be active and assertive. We should feel free to ask questions: Is this medication necessary? What is it supposed to do? What side effects might it have? Is surgery really necessary? How about a second opinion? Is hospitalization necessary or could treatment be provided on an outpatient basis?

While some physicians may resent being questioned, many are coming to recognize that patients are capable of collaborating in their own healing. Patients can do that only as they dispel the sacral mystique with which we have surrounded the practice of medicine. Those whose faith is in the Lord of creation will not place that faith in fallible human beings or institutions, recognizing that at their best those agents are instruments for the healing power which comes from God alone.

PROLONGING LIFE AND FACING DEATH

Death provides the ultimate test of our faith. In the power of his resurrection, Christ has overcome the sting of death and has opened to us the gates of everlasting life. The last enemy has been destroyed.

But death is still an enemy. We all face certain death; there is no way out for us. But if we believe the promise of the Gospel, we can face death with courage and hope. How we die, then, can be just as important as how we live.

Modern medical practice is based on assumptions far removed from the Christian conviction about God as Lord of life. For the medical community, death is the ultimate antagonist which must be kept at bay at all costs, using whatever means are available. Many physicians find it hard to let go and accept the fact that their patient will die despite all that they may do.

At best this attitude has led to the development of techniques that have enabled people to survive serious illnesses that once would have claimed their lives: transfusions, intravenous feeding, heart massage, microsurgery, heart/lung machines, new forms of resuscitation. At worst, however, this same attitude has led some physicians to subject dying patients to all sorts of traumas and indignities just to prolong life by a few days, even though those days are spent in pain or unconsciousness.

We have recently begun to question whether life should be indefinitely prolonged by artificial means. Religious people are beginning to concede that artificial life-support systems should be removed when it becomes clear that a comatose patient has no reasonable chance of reviving. Even the legal definition of death is undergoing revision because the heart can be kept beating long after the brain has ceased to function.

Just as in ordinary treatment, in these critical situations we need to take an active part in the decisions about what is to be done. Should radical surgery be performed to enable the patient to live for a few more days? Or should the patient discontinue treatment, leave the hospital, and go home to die?

Recently there has been a movement to encourage people to sign a "living will" which requests that no heroic measures be taken to prolong life. If the person is in a coma, the living will can be used to authorize the attending physician to discontinue radical treatments. Thus individuals can make their wishes known before the event, so that others can act on those wishes if the person is unable to make them known.

How should we treat other people who are terminally ill? We have become much more frank and open about death than we once were. Too often in the past, Christians, like everyone else, have tended to hide from a terminal patient the full extent of the illness, pretending—"Of course you'll get well"—even when recovery was out of the question.

Physicians today are more willing to share with patients the real truth about their condition, even when they are terminally ill. Of course this can be overdone; it should be done only if the patient is able to bear the news and if it can be done in such a way as not to foreclose all hope prematurely. Conveyed with love and support, the full truth can enable the sick person to prepare for death.

Family and friends can be most helpful if they cooperate with the medical team so that the patient is not besieged with conflicting messages. They can help the patient talk about his condition and his feelings about it. They can call in a priest before the patient is beyond the capacity to communicate.

The hospice movement, just now getting under way in this country, offers a new possibility for terminal care outside the traditional hospital. The hospice works only with dying patients; it provides care rather than therapy. It provides a supportive, homelike environment where the patient can be made comfortable, free of pain, and accessible to friends and family.

While there is nothing to be gained from a morbid preoccupation with death, there is nevertheless much that thoughtful Christians can do to prepare themselves and their families for death when it does come. They can talk about it together, airing their attitudes and expressing their wishes about what they would want done, should they be unable to do it for themselves.

If I were in a coma with no hope of regaining consciousness, what would I want to have happen? What provisions for terminal care would I prefer? What are my wishes about burial? Cremation? Funeral arrangements? By looking with honesty and clarity at these issues before they become matters for immediate decision, we can help ourselves and those around us to prepare for death when it comes.

While we cannot examine every ethical issue involved in the field of medicine, on the basis of those few we have discussed, we can see some common Christian convictions underlying our attitude and our responses to matters of life and health, sickness and death.

We want to be healthy, but our desire for health is tempered by our knowledge that life inevitably brings sickness as well. So while we take proper care of our bodies, as good stewards should, we do not make a fetish of health, nor will we plague the physicians on the assumption that they can keep us free from all disease and pain. We fight death as an enemy, but we recognize that, in God's good time, it must come. We alone can take responsibility for deciding how we will meet it.

· 11 ·

Ethics in the
Economic Sphere

Economic activity has profound moral significance because it directly affects the quality of human life. It has to do with how we earn our living, what we can buy and own, what pleasures we can pursue. It determines whether or not there will be justice in the society, whether people will be exploited, whether some will be very rich and others very poor.

Economic decisions are matters of human choice in which our values come into play. Those choices must, therefore, be subjected to ethical inquiry: Are they consistent with God's will for his people? Do they help us to meet God's demand for love and justice for all?

At the same time, economic decisions are made within certain constraints. "The bottom line"—so revered by the commercial mind—is a reality not to be ignored. Economic plans and proposals, no matter how ethically sensitive, must conform to the demands of the balance sheet. There is no moral superiority in driving a business—or a whole economy—into ruin.

That fact is often used as an excuse for avoiding moral issues in the marketplace. Bribery, misrepresentation, kick-backs, price fixing, stock manipulation, and other evils are justified on the ground that "Everybody does it, so you have to do it to survive."

Those who seek easy alibis for their conduct may be

165

satisfied with such evasions, but those who are genuinely concerned about the moral climate of business life will want to probe more deeply into the issues. Let us look, then, at some areas in which the Christian moral vision might affect the economic sphere.

The Economic System

Economic activity is carried on within the context of a particular economic system. For us in America, that system is capitalism, which is based on certain assumptions about economic behavior.

In the capitalist model, individuals pool their savings to invest in business enterprises. The price of goods varies in response to the forces of supply and demand within a free, self-regulating market. Competition assures that the public interest will be served, as the less efficient producers will be forced out of business. The energy for the system is supplied by the insatiable desire of economic man for more goods and services.

That is the theory, but it has not worked out quite that way in practice. Competition, far from providing balance, turns out to be a developmental force, leaving only a few large companies surviving over the long haul. Cooperation rather than competition sets prices and splits up the market. Economic man's wants are not insatiable; they have to be stimulated by advertising.

Finally, the private pursuit of selfish gain does not always yield the public interest. Shoddy or even dangerous products may bring in larger profits; if so, they will probably be made and sold. Unless the purchasers are very sophisticated in evaluating highly complicated products, they will never be the wiser.

Capitalism has scored some impressive successes. It has provided an amazing diversity of industrial products, often at very low cost. It has stimulated invention and organizational creativity. It has provided a high level of prosperity and living standards for large numbers of people.

On the other hand, capitalism has been unable to provide economic stability for long periods of time. Cycles of boom and bust have created havoc and disruption. Nor does capitalism provide those services which are socially necessary but not economically profitable: the postal service, for example, or mass public transportation.

Capitalism has not provided employment for all. Indeed many economists believe that it requires a measure of unemployment to provide flexibility in the system. Thus capitalism has failed to provide an adequate level of social justice. Not only does it permit vast discrepancies between wealth and poverty, but may even require a permanent under-class of exploited poor in order to survive.

In the light of these failures, can capitalism be reconciled with the Christian moral vision with its concern for social justice, human solidarity, and personal freedom? Many Christian thinkers have answered No and have espoused socialism as an alternative.

Socialism, though not of the Marxist variety, has been advocated by many of the leading theologians of the Anglican tradition, from Frederick D. Maurice to William Temple. They were persuaded by the socialist commitment to corporate values over individualistic values, which seemed more in harmony with the Christian commitment to human solidarity. They approved of the socialist emphasis on cooperation rather than conflict. They especially valued socialism's dictum: production for use, not for profit.

But our historical experience with socialism has not been too encouraging. In democratic socialist countries like Great Britain it turns out to make little difference to the worker whether the coal mine is owned privately or publicly. Economic unrest has been mitigated but it has not disappeared. Socialist governments seem to act very much like capitalist employers when profits, costs, labor relations, and interest rates are at stake.

Marxist countries have been more rigorous in their economic planning, but at the cost of human freedom. When the state is the sole economic agency, the private person has no alternative. When economic planning has the force of law, the worker can be forced to remain at the job, robbed of the freedom to move.

In a socialist economy, goods are produced according to what some official agency deems necessary, not according to the wishes of the consumer. Economics and politics are so closely intertwined that economic disagreements become political dissent and cannot be tolerated because of the need for national unity.

Neither capitalism nor socialism fully embodies Christian moral values. Capitalism more effectively promotes human freedom, while socialism is more likely to produce equality and social justice. Capitalism is more dynamic, socialism more stable, but neither system enjoys any clear moral superiority.

Christians, therefore, can conscientiously espouse either capitalism or socialism, but not without some misgivings. Most of us will be content to live and work within the confines of the system we have inherited, subjecting that system to a continuing moral critique from the perspective of the Christian vision of the good society. Should the time come when the entire system appears to be beyond redemption, then we will be justified in seeking to overthrow it in favor of another.

We in the United States have inherited an economic system that is basically capitalist. It is full of contradictions and has produced more than its share of instability and injustice. Many wise and perceptive observers claim that its days are numbered. I do not, however, believe that is the case. I rather expect that most of us now living will end our days still under some form of capitalism. Furthermore I believe we can affirm the basic system and work for reform and renewal without overturning or replacing the system itself.

At the same time, we should respect those peoples who have opted for other economic systems. Some societies, for example, have adopted the socialist model of economic life. We can claim no moral superiority over them, merely because we maintain a different economic system. Neither one is necessarily more Christian than the other.

Government Regulation of the Economy

The plain fact is that the capitalist system has never existed in its pure theoretical form. We have been constantly experimenting with it from the beginning. Even price-fixing, not entirely unknown in the business world today, is a primitive form of economic planning. Government intervention in the economy, though vigorously opposed by business spokesmen, has been a constant in American history; the system probably could not have survived without it.

We hear a great deal about the need to get the government out of the economy, but most of that rhetoric is beside the point. In a complex technological society such as ours, government involvement in the economy is beyond being desirable or undesirable; it is inevitable.

Most governmental regulation of business came about because it was necessary for the common good. It has not been a liberal or conservative issue. Both political parties have, at one time or another, sponsored efforts to regulate some sector of the economy.

Pure food and drug laws, for example, were passed in order to insure that people were not being sold harmful substances. The laws were needed because many contaminated foods and untested drugs were being marketed. The securities market in America was subjected to regulation after the stock market crash of 1929. As a result, people who buy stocks and bonds now have some assurance that their holdings are what they claim to be. Today many banks proudly advertise the fact that deposits are insured by an agency of the federal government.

Government regulation helps to insure safety in the product and in the work place. Accidents, disease, and death still exact a significant toll in the work force. Product safety is still a major issue, as the numerous recalls of defective automobiles testifies. Government requires truth in advertising and equal opportunity in employment, all objectives which a responsible Christian would support.

These objectives could never be achieved without the coercive power of government. Not even the most conscientious business executives could afford to install expensive safety devices or insure a high standard of purity in a food product, because their less conscientious competitors would then enjoy a competitive edge. But when purity and safety standards are required by law, all companies have to comply. Public policy, then, is supporting the most conscientious employers, who could never afford to act on their own.

Complaints about overregulation are certainly valid. There are too many regulations, many of them difficult to obey and to enforce, others arbitrary and useless. The whole area of administrative law is far removed from public scrutiny and the discipline of the democratic process. A massive overhaul of regulations and regulatory agencies is surely in order, a move that would answer the complaints of many business executives who have to conform to their demands.

At the same time, the opposite complaint is heard, namely that the regulators get too cosy with those they are supposed to regulate. It is easy to see how this happens. Regulatory officials are chosen for their knowledge of the field to be regulated. Thus they are often people who have worked closely with the very companies they are supposed to monitor.

What is even more questionable, many officials seek employment with those same companies after their period of government service is over. Like the unjust steward in Jesus' parable, they are tempted to make friends with unrighteous Mammon by being excessively lenient toward the offenses of the companies that come under their purview. This "revolving door" between government and business employment is an open door to corruption and needs to be closely watched.

Thus the regulatory practices of government have their problems, but the system needs to be scrutinized and evaluated on the basis of facts, not meaningless rhetoric about government interference.

The Moral Status of Economic Growth

For the foreseeable future, we will continue to have a mixed sort of economy with business and government coexisting in an uneasy partnership, in which most of us participate merely as consumers and citizens. Some of the ethical issues generated by this arrangement are of such large scale that we can do little to affect them, yet we have a stake in the outcome. The first of these is the issue of economic growth itself.

A major debate has erupted over the question of economic growth. How much growth is possible? How much is desirable? Some argue that an ever-expanding economy eats into scarce resources and hastens their exhaustion. In the interest of future generations, we should put on the brakes and learn to live with a no-growth economy.

Others argue that, even aside from the problem of resources, our commitment to continued economic expansion can only increase the pollution of air and water as we resort to less clean forms of energy in order to increase production. Thus it is wrong to expand the economy just to increase our own prosperity.

But it is also clear that if we are to eliminate poverty and unemployment, if the disadvantaged minorities and other outsiders are to be brought into the circle of prosperity, the economy will have to expand to make more jobs available. And if the developing nations are to reach their own goals of providing a decent standard of living for their people, the world economy will have to expand many times over in the years to come. The price for slow growth is paid by the poor. Their welfare requires economic growth.

One answer to the question of resource depletion is that a sophisticated economy like ours does not expand only by making more things, thereby using up more materials and energy. Ours has become a service-oriented economy. Most of our growth is in the nonmaterial sector, which does not necessarily require the use of more natural resources.

The case can be made that economic growth is essential, though the amount of growth may remain in dispute. The ethical issue has to do with the kind of growth we are to have and who is to benefit from it. Christians would maintain that economic growth should be accompanied by an increase in social justice, by widening opportunities for the poor, the outsiders, and the oppressed. In the long run, our society will be judged on the basis of its ability to eliminate poverty and oppression and to provide a reasonably good life for all, free from want and deprivation.

Our National Product: What Shall We Make?

A moral critique of our economy must consider not only the question of growth but also the nature of that growth. If it is good to have a larger gross national product, it is important to ask just what constitutes that product. What do we want our economy to provide for us? As consumers, what do we want to consume? If economic growth merely means more cosmetics, more deodorants, more fur-lined can openers, if it means style changes that make our automobiles obsolete every three years, then we ought to raise some serious questions about the direction we are taking.

The producer, with some justification, will say, "I don't decide what to make. I just give the public what they want." That is true, but only up to a point. That same producer will spend millions of dollars on advertising to create a non-existent need. Who needs another brand of soap? Another breakfast food? A double-swivel disposable razor? As the consuming public, we do as we are told, but is that inevitable? Perhaps Christians can begin to influence the economic scene by becoming more intentional about our own economic behavior.

Economists speak of "goods" and "services," about the "standard of living." All are theological terms. What are the real goods of this life? What would constitute a genuinely Christian standard of living?

Christian stewardship means more than merely giving money to the church. It means the responsible use of the resources that God has entrusted to us. That makes it important for us to ask: What do we really want and need? What can we do without? How can we keep from getting sucked into the mindless pursuit of the next thing? How can we stay free of the manipulators and make responsible choices about the use of our economic resources?

To ask these questions does not imply that Christians

should not buy and consume. It means that we should look responsibly at our own economic behavior. It means developing some convictions about what we regard as the goods of life. It means being self-conscious about our own standard of living.

Our individual choices will certainly not alter the course of the American economy. But as more and more of us begin to consider these issues and make responsible choices, we may have some corporate effect on the development of an economy that is just and humane, careful of the physical resources that God has given us, thoughtful of the natural environment in which it all takes place.

Moral Responsibility of the Company

Anyone looking at the working of our economic system must come to terms with the profit motive. The idea of profitability is certainly justifiable. It applies to socialist as well as to capitalist enterprises. Even nonprofit organizations have to break even in order to survive. Businesses have to make profits so that they can pay their investors a return on their investment. It is hard to argue against these functions of profits.

The more serious issues arise when investors seek the highest possible rate of return. Consider a small apartment complex which serves a modest income group. It is functioning well, making a decent return on the owners' investment. But it is in a very desirable location, one highly sought after by developers who want to build a high-rise luxury apartment building. Because of the favorable location, they can make a great deal of money.

The ethical issue here is not profits, for the existing apartments are already making a decent profit. The issue is the maximization of profits. The pursuit of bigger bucks will mean the destruction of the apartment complex, the dispersal of tenants, a decline in housing for people of modest means, and an influx of the wealthy. In many of our large cities, this story is being repeated over and over again.

The matter is complicated by the divorce of ownership

from management in corporate life. We once saw this change as a blessing. In the bad old days, businesses were run by greedy entrepreneurs—robber barons—who were tough and mean and ran their businesses with an iron hand, exploiting people in the process. But as stock holding became more diversified, management passed into the hands of a new breed of professional managers who themselves held only small amounts of company stock.

These new managers were merely employees, though very highly paid ones. They brought rational, scientific methods to the conduct of business. They were seen as less arbitrary, more civilized and humane than the older generation of owner-managers. Management was thus divorced from greed and profits.

But was it? The manager is still responsible to the stock holders. Now that they themselves are no longer involved in the making and selling of the product, their only interest is in the profit-and-loss statement: the bottom line.

So if the manager cannot deliver adequate profits, out he goes. If company profits seem to lag regardless of management, the company itself can be scuttled and the money invested more profitably somewhere else. A plant may be closed, workers laid off, communities put through a crisis as a result of decisions made far away by people who may not even be aware of the distress they have caused.

Who are these owners? Not the widows and orphans of company propaganda, perhaps, but not a collection of filthy rich capitalists either. More and more stock is owned by other corporate bodies: pension plans, insurance companies, banks, universities, and even church agencies.

Those who manage such funds see themselves as working to provide support for good causes. Of course they want those funds to earn maximum profits. They would be poor stewards if they did not. So perhaps unwittingly, economic decisions that have disastrous repercussions are often made in the interest of lofty purposes.

Some churches have begun to study this matter of social responsibility in investment policy. The Episcopal Church's General Convention has appointed a committee to make recommendations in this area for the benefit of trustees of all church-related funds. Some investments have been changed in response to these recommendations. In other cases, church bodies have exercised their rights as stockholders to demand changes in company policies in the direction of greater social responsibility. These efforts show a commendable interest in introducing other elements than mere profits into the investment picture. They may set an example for other conscientious investors in the future.

Moral Responsibility to the Company

In addition to our concern for the moral quality of corporate actions, we also need to look at our moral responsibility to the business organization as well. Statistics indicate that every year businesses lose millions of dollars through employee pilfering, padded expense accounts, shoplifting, kickbacks and similar activities. Many people who would never think of actually stealing anything find themselves doing such things without regarding their actions as morally significant.

But theft is theft, whether it takes the form of stealing the last dollar from a poor blind man or taking pens from the supply cabinet of a soulless corporation—or from the government, which is the favored victim in my hometown.

It is always easy to justify such rip-offs. They're covered by insurance. It will never be missed. They underpay me anyhow. Well, they cheat people too! All such rationalizations only help us deceive ourselves about the nature of our actions.

We need to raise the level of our consciousness about the moral quality of such actions. We will be in a better position to demand morally responsible conduct from the company when we behave more responsibly to the company.

The Labor Union Movement

No treatment of our economic system would be adequate without some discussion of the labor movement. Labor unions have had a difficult time establishing their legitimacy in the eyes of mainline church members. With our highly individualistic orientation, we have tended to see industry as the private concern of the factory owner. From that perspective, people have reasoned that, of course the owner should be allowed to pay his employees whatever he wants. If they don't like it, they can always go somewhere else to work. The law enforced this theory by regarding unions as conspiracies in restraint of trade. Courts regularly issued injunctions to prevent the calling of a strike or to inhibit union leaders' activities when a strike was called.

Some churches took a contrary view. In the Episcopal Church, a pro-union organization called the Church Association for the Advancement of the Interests of Labor included many bishops, clergy, and lay leaders. These union supporters argued that workers had a right to band together to negotiate with management for more just treatment in the form of better pay and better working conditions.

During the New Deal period, Congress adopted labor legislation which gave workers the right to organize, to vote for union representation, and to bargain collectively with their employers. Since that time unions have become a powerful and permanent part of the American economic scene.

Their record has been impressive. The American worker today is perhaps the best paid in the world. Rising labor costs have induced employers to make full use of labor-saving machinery, thereby increasing worker productivity. Higher wages transform workers into consumers. Thus the union movement has been partly responsible for the amazing growth of the American economy after World War II.

Many conscientious people still raise questions about the legitimacy of the labor unions. They seem too powerful. Their wage demands are frequently inflationary. The strongest unions can deliver the highest benefits to their members, whether deserved or not. Workers are often required to join unions against their will.

Some unions are shot through with corruption, their leaders predatory and sometimes allied with organized crime. Others practice racial discrimination. Featherbedding—the requirement that a company retain unneeded workers—is widespread in industries making major technological innovations. As more and more public employees become unionized, strikes interrupt public services, causing great inconvenience to many who have no influence over the bargaining process.

These criticisms certainly need to be taken seriously. Union reform is an urgent necessity, given the power of the union in both industry and government. But there is no doubt that unions represent legitimate expressions of the corporate concerns of American workers. They have helped to keep workers content to remain within the confines of the capitalist system, even when that system seems to be in deep trouble. They have conferred a measure of dignity upon the worker who can assert, through the union, the right to bargain on equal terms with the employer.

Union members feel that the churches have a built-in bias against unions. Most lay leaders of the churches come from the employer, rather than the worker, class. Most clergy come from middle-class backgrounds with little knowledge of or sympathy with factory workers, truck drivers, or longshoremen. They tend to blame strikes on the union leaders who call out the workers, and they fail to see that a strike represents a breakdown in the negotiation process, a failure which should be borne by both participants.

If church members can accept the legitimacy of the union and its collective bargaining function, they will be in a better position to see the ethical issues involved in any particular labor dispute instead of prejudging the case in favor of the employer, as has frequently been the case in the past.

A Christian Perspective on Work

The major contribution that most of us make to economic society is the work we do. We work because we must. Some of us like our jobs; some do not. But in either case, we seldom look at our work from a theological perspective. If there is a biblical doctrine of work, what would it be?

The curse of Adam comes immediately to mind. In the Genesis story, when God discovers that Adam and Eve have eaten the forbidden fruit, he throws them out of the garden, saying to Adam, "In the sweat of thy face shalt thou eat bread" (3:19). To the ancient world, that meant that work was something you just had to endure, like it or not. It was a rather negative view of work, but a realistic one at least.

But Genesis offers another way of looking at work. At the end of the six days of creation, after God has made the world and all that is in it, "God saw everything he had made, and behold, it was very good" (1:31).

That text suggests that God himself is a worker, a creator. We who are made in his image are called to be workers too. Work, then, is not just what we do to earn our bread. It is how we imitate God. God works; we work. God expresses himself through his creation; we express ourselves through our work.

We are called to be workers. The theological term for this call is "vocation." Secular society uses the word vocation as a synonym for work, but in the Christian vocabulary it means much more. The doctrine of vocation asserts that God calls each one of us to serve him and his people in some particular way. The work we do, whether in a paying job, a volunteer capacity, or in running a home, is our response to God's call to us.

Our work, then, is what God has called us to do. It is the way in which we exercise our God-given creativity. That being the case, there are some important things to be said about the right to work, our attitude toward work, and the quality of our work life.

THE RIGHT TO WORK

Since work is one of the ways in which we express our basic humanity, then it follows that all of God's children should have a chance to work. Translated into terms of social policy, it means that the society itself has an obligation to provide work for everyone.

Today there are simply not enough jobs to go around. That is the human meaning of those bloodless statistics we read about unemployment. Millions of people are looking for work but are unable to find it.

Some people believe that others are unemployed because they do not want to work. That may be true of some people but not of most. Most unemployed people would prefer to work if given a chance. The trouble is that they do not get the chance.

How does a society go about making jobs available for all? That is a matter of strategy about which reasonable people differ sharply. Liberals think that government should create jobs, acting as an employer of last resort. Conservatives tend to favor incentives to encourage business expansion that will open up jobs without government getting into the act. Whichever way turns out to be most feasible, the important thing is that we as a nation accept the responsibility for seeing that, some way or other, more people get a chance to work.

CREATIVITY IN WORK

For those of us who have jobs, it is important that we learn to express our creativity and imagination through our work. That is easier, of course, if the job is a glamorous one, if it is well regarded and well paid. But nearly any job, no matter how menial, can be a source of personal pride for the worker and gratification for those with whom the worker comes into contact.

I think about my own dealings with sales people in stores, the checker at the supermarket, the mail carrier, the government clerk where I get my driver's license. Most of them are alert, energetic, courteous, and interested in what they are doing. When that is the case, the contact is pleasant and refreshing. But sometimes I encounter someone who is so mean, grouchy, vague, or sloppy, that my whole day is spoiled.

I wonder about the difference between those two sorts of people. How different is their effect on other people. How different their own lives must be.

Most people are justifiably suspicious when someone says, "Be happy in your work." It sounds like managerial propaganda or the simpering sentimentality of professional Pollyannas. But I am concerned primarily with the way in which we ourselves are affected by our attitude toward our work.

If we see our work as a vocation, we will work in such a way as to serve God and his people. Our work thus becomes a form of ministry that affects the lives of countless others. For ourselves, the most important thing we get in return is not our paycheck but our self-respect, our pride of accomplishment. Our work can enable us to express that creative urge within ourselves that is the image of God himself.

THE QUALITY OF WORK LIFE

But some jobs are hard to get excited about. Some are dull and boring. Some are sheer drudgery. Many people work in drab and cheerless surroundings. In some cases the unpleasantness is inherent in the job. Where that is true, perhaps those workers should be paid unusually well, since in a capitalist society money represents the most sincere form of affirmation.

In far too many instances, work is made unpleasant by stupid rules and customs, the insensitivity of employers and supervisors, the pettiness of fellow workers, the inconsiderateness of the public. If people are to be enabled to express their creativity in their work, then work should be made as pleasant and congenial as possible.

Employers bear most of the burden of creating attractive conditions on the job. Some companies have already done such things as eliminating the time clock, allowing employees to choose their hours of work and to schedule their own activities. This innovation gives workers a sense of personal responsibility for their work. It enables them to choose the hours when they can do their best work. This arrangement is especially helpful to working mothers, who want to be home when their children need them.

Some employers are beginning to make better use of part-time workers. Part-time employment may achieve major importance in the years to come, as the number of two-career families increases. Women with children can work part time and produce an income without disrupting family life. Business gains access to a new constituency of potential employees.

If the promise of part-time employment is to be realized, employers will have to take better care of their part-time workers. Up to now, our institutions have treated them as second-class citizens. They seldom qualify for fringe benefits. They get no vacations. They are seldom considered for promotions.

Another innovation is the attempt to find alternatives to the traditional assembly line. In some factories, a production team will make an entire product, a feature that takes much of the drudgery out of factory work. Though still in its infancy, this development promises to close the gap between the worker and the product. In assembly-line work, the operator might not even know how his own piece of the work fitted into the finished product.

The value of these changes is that they show an understanding of the importance of work as a human activity. Work is not just the way people earn a living; it is the way they spend most of their lives, the way they express their intelligence and their creative imagination. It is the way they imitate God, the divine creator.

YOUNG PEOPLE AND WORK

The continuity of any social system depends upon its ability to induct a rising generation of young people into their adult social roles. Learning to work is perhaps the most important of the functions that transform the child into the adult.

Our society is experiencing difficulty in carrying off this transition. Our young people do not understand work. They find it strange, remote, forbidding. As a result, they often find it hard to break into the working life.

Some people believe that this is true because our young people are pampered and overindulged. They simply do not want to leave their pleasant childish pursuits to take on adult responsibilities. But the facts are more complex. Our young people grow up without ever seeing people do the kind of work with which they would identify themselves.

Children who come from very poor families may grow up surrounded by nonworking adults. They may know only welfare mothers, unemployed men, and teen-agers who have never held a job. It is hard for such children to picture themselves in a working role. They have no experience with demands to report for duty with regularity, to appear on time, to keep the customers satisfied, or to perform up to expected standards.

Middle-class children may have both parents working regularly but still not know very much about what they actually do. When asked about their parents' work, they may reply, "My dad's in insurance," or "My mother works for HEW." But these are merely job titles and organizational names. They tell little about what the person actually does. The job itself may be impossible to explain to a child. Can you say something more than, "I push papers around?"

Paul Goodman once suggested that our compulsory education and child labor laws have worked to isolate young people from the world of work. Goodman recommended greater use of work/study programs that would enable high school students to gain experience in the working environment. They could see the kinds of jobs that people actually do and could learn what is involved in doing them. They could learn some of the disciplines of working life: what it takes to hold a job. They could earn pocket money and achieve a sense of dignity and usefulness. Lost school time could be made up by courses that relate to their jobs or open the way to advancement.

The evidence does not suggest that the rising generation of young people is either lazy or unwilling to work. The society has a corporate responsibility to find more ways to introduce young people to meaningful work, to give them access to work worth doing. Only then can they be expected to find their way smoothly into the productive world of adulthood.

Leisure

One of the greatest benefits of our economic system has been its ability to make leisure time available to most workers. The forty-hour work week leaves evenings and weekends free. Paid vacations are commonplace. Retirement is available at age sixty-five, or younger in some systems. All of these factors increase the availability of free time that we can use as we see fit.

The benefits of leisure are obvious; the difficulties it raises are less obvious but nonetheless real. Many people in our society are programed for work and do not know how to get along without it. When given free time, they are bored and can only "kill time" or engage in frantic activity, often spending a great deal of money in the process.

For many people, it is their work which has given meaning and significance to their lives. When retirement comes and that work is taken from them, life loses its meaning. They feel cut adrift, left out of things, depressed, and often angry. Sometimes they simply vegetate, go into an early decline, suffer illness and even death.

Leisure, then, is a moral issue, one that illustrates the difficulty of asserting a value while affirming a contrary value at the same time. Thus Christians would claim that work is good because it is a vocation. God calls us to serve him in our work and to exercise our creativity in imitation of him.

At the same time, we would claim that leisure is also good. It is also a calling. It also affords an opportunity to express our creativity. In leisure we also imitate God who, after he had created the world, rested on the seventh day.

The difficulty posed by leisure is that if we have always functioned within constraints, we may find it hard to function without them. On the job we are always under the demands of the clock, the calendar, the measurement of our output. In leisure we have to decide these things for ourselves. We have to determine how we will spend our time.

The most terrifying aspect of leisure is that there is nothing that we must do. In leisure God calls us, not to do but to be.

The call to being requires that we look at the world in a new way. It enables us to see aspects of life that escape us as long as we are on the run.

Since leisure is such a new experience for many of us, we have to learn how to handle it. We cannot afford to wait until retirement comes, for by that time, we may be too set in our ways to be able to change easily. Vacations give us a chance to practice leisure. Weekends give us a brief sample of it. We can use those occasions for our training in being, not doing.

Some people train for it by doing something quite different from what they do at work. Thus an accountant may go sailing, a typist go skiing. A busy salesman may settle down with a book, a professor build furniture. Such activities introduce into our lives elements that we would normally lack. We do them for the sheer pleasure of the doing. No results are necessary.

As we become more skilled in our use of leisure time, we may find it less important to do anything at all. We may find ourselves able to back off from doing and simply be, with pleasure. We can enter into the spirit of divine play. That is the true meaning of the Sabbath: no work, nothing useful.

Leisure may thus be the most important achievement of civilization, the most significant product of economic activity. It would be a tragic waste if we worked so hard to make it available that we were unable to enjoy it when we achieve it.

· 12 ·

―――――

Moral Aspects
of Political Life

―――――

Many Christians who would acknowledge the relevance of
the Christian moral vision in the social and economic realm
would nevertheless confess to having difficulty in relating
their Christian faith to the world of politics. Politics is, after
all, rather messy business at times. It deals with power and
coercion, compromise and corruption. Politics is divisive. It
deals with controversial matters, often in an atmosphere of
bitterness and vindictiveness. In such an atmosphere, legitimate moral concerns tend to get sidetracked.

Similar difficulties are cited from the political side by those
who would prefer to keep politics an autonomous sphere,
free from any outside influences. Considerations of power
and expediency, group or national interest, are the proper
ingredients of politics according to this view. When religious
groups and individuals get into the political act, they contaminate it by introducing extraneous moral considerations.
Religious people are regarded as naïve, otherworldly do-
gooders who do not understand the rules of the political game
and who therefore do more harm than good.

We can concede the legitimacy of these complaints. Politics
can be divisive, destroying harmony and breaking fellowship. Church groups often do get into the political power
game, with disastrous results. Religious people can be naïve
and simplistic, ignoring the realities of the political situation.

But any version of Christianity that fails to encompass the

political sphere is untrue to the biblical heritage. Biblical concern for politics is most evident in the Old Testament, of course, for Israel was both a covenant community and a national state. Visionary prophets instructed kings and even condemned them. Activist prophets participated in palace intrigues and even helped to lead revolutions. In Israel, government functioned under the law of God, who was the true King of Israel.

In the New Testament, Israel is no longer an independent state but a subjugated people, yet political concern is still evident. When Jesus said, "Render therefore to Caesar the things that are Caesar's, and to God the things that are God's" (Mt. 22:21), he was making a political statement. The individual has an obligation to support the government within its proper sphere, but that sphere is limited in the demands it can lay upon the citizen.

Paul says essentially the same thing: "Let every person be subject to the governing authorities. For there is no authority except from God and those that exist have been instituted by God" (Rom. 13:1). This passage has often been used to justify an uncritical obedience on the part of the individual, but that is not necessarily the best reading of Paul. He emphasizes the role of the subject because he is writing to Christians. The phrase, ". . . there is no authority except from God" reminds the ruler that he governs, not by his own authority but under the authority of God, whom he, too, is obligated to obey.

God's lordship over all of life extends to the realm of politics, where public policy is formed to deal with issues which have moral and spiritual implications. Christians, therefore, should be aware of how their religious commitment affects their political stance.

The Purpose of Government

Christian political thought has identified both a negative and a positive function of government. The negative function is the suppression of evil; the positive is the enhancement of human life.

Paul proclaims the negative function: "He [the ruler] is the servant of God to execute his wrath on the evil doer" (Rom. 13:4). While this sounds rather harsh, it means merely that the first function of government is to establish order, without which all the other blessings of civil life are impossible. The preservation of order requires the ability to control the population to prevent uprising and chaos. It requires the ability to repel invaders, external threats to the good order of the community. Our own Constitution, in its preamble, states both of these purposes succinctly: ". . . insure domestic tranquillity, provide for the common defence."

The basic requirement for the enhancement of life is the provision of justice, which also has a positive and a negative aspect. Negative justice means that conflicting claims are adjudicated by a neutral third force, the civil power. Justice is blind—it is no respecter of persons. It seeks to achieve balance, fairness, impartiality.

On the positive side, justice means that all people have access to the goods and services of the community so that no one is hungry, deprived, or exploited. This distributive justice is not blind; it is biased in favor of the poor, the outcast, the loser. Again, our Constitution has recognized these purposes of the state in the phrases, "establish justice" and "promote the general welfare."

Finally, government should provide a context in which people can fulfill their own legitimate purposes, free from arbitrary control or restriction. Even the power of the state must be restrained to enable private purposes to flourish. Again our Constitution includes a reference to this value: "to secure the blessings of liberty to ourselves and our posterity."

The Framework of Politics: Democracy

Our concern with politics takes place within our own historical framework, the American political system. That system is democratic in character, though it partakes of some characteristics that are hard to classify.

When democracy first appeared on the modern scene, most of the church opposed it. Christians had long become accustomed to rule by the privileged: a monarch of royal blood, assisted by a hereditary nobility. The alliance of throne and altar had been cemented by centuries of experience; democracy seemed a dangerous innovation that Christians would do well to avoid.

The hostility of the church was sharpened by the fact that many proponents of democracy were religiously unorthodox. Some were deists, some agnostic, some openly atheist. Even those who professed Christianity were often opposed to the church, which was regarded as a bastion of privilege which must be overthrown.

There were also theological grounds for this suspicion of democracy. It appealed to a heretical doctrine of man, one that claimed that man is inherently good and that only traditional institutions are responsible for human corruption. Once those institutions were overthrown, a new golden age would follow. The will of the people, the majority, can be trusted with complete authority.

Christians who hold to the doctrine of original sin cannot accept this view. Augustine was right to see that human propensity for evil has to be kept in check, by force if necessary. Government will always be necessary to keep people under control.

The Augustinian view validated the whole apparatus of political authority: monarchy, hierarchy, custom and tradition, law and coercive power, all of which hedge mankind about and make civil society possible. The mass is not to be trusted; it is dangerous and unruly. Given this view of humanity, it is no wonder that most orthodox Christians opposed the coming of the democratic idea.

But democracy came nevertheless and Christians accommodated to it, often without much theoretical support. But some Christian thinkers were able to spot the flaw in the argument that led from original sin to authoritarian government. The traditional argument asserts the sinfulness of all people, but then produces, like a rabbit out of a hat, a race of trustworthy governors in the persons of kings and nobles. A consistent doctrine of human sinfulness would declare that these people, too, are sinful and not to be trusted.

Thomas Jefferson pointed out this flaw in his first inaugural address:

> Sometimes it is said that man cannot be trusted with the government of himself. Can he, then, be trusted with the government of others? Or have we found angels in the form of kings to govern him?[1]

Thus the idea of original sin, far from undercutting the concept of democracy, serves to support it, as Reinhold Niebuhr noted:

> Man's capacity for justice makes democracy possible; but man's inclination to injustice makes democracy necessary.[2]

Our political system is committed to democracy, but with a cautious and tentative attitude. We affirm majority rule, but hedge it about with qualifications to insure the rights of minorities. There are some things that even an overwhelming majority of voters cannot do. They cannot abrogate the Bill of Rights. Devices such as representative government, the separation of powers, the federal system, help to restrain the majority of the moment.

The central affirmation of democracy is human equality. While all democratic societies share that value, they do not all agree on its meaning. At the very least, it means that all citizens should be equally treated by the government, that they have equal standing before the courts. For us it has come to mean that defendants in criminal cases should be provided with free legal assistance if they cannot afford it themselves. It also means that segregation and discrimination in hiring and promotion practices are deemed illegal.

As the concept of equality develops in a changing society, each new application of the idea becomes a battleground for conflicting forces. Our most recent such conflict centers around affirmative action programs which seek to overcome the results of past discriminatory practices by providing special avenues of access to jobs and education by black people and other minority groups.

The movement to complete the guarantee of equal rights for women has been even more controversial. It is difficult to see why a constitutional amendment to insure those rights should be a matter of such controversy in a society that sees itself as committed to equality. Fear of the loss of traditional privileges, or uncertainty as to what would result from the Equal Rights Amendment are probably the reasons for the opposition. It would be a curious irony if the nation were to find itself unable to make a clear constitutional commitment to women's rights after two centuries of trail-blazing work in making human equality a living reality.

Along with the democratic revolution has come the rise of the secular state. This development has meant a loss of privilege for the church, but a gain in freedom from political influence. Thus while the Episcopal Church and the Church of England share the same doctrine of episcopacy, the two churches function quite differently. The Episcopal Church chooses its bishops by clergy and laity acting jointly in open convention. In England, bishops are still appointed by the Crown, usually on the advice of the Prime Minister. Though this latter system has produced many able and dedicated bishops, their appointments are essentially political acts over which church members have no control.

A religiously diverse nation requires a religiously neutral state. It is not required to be antireligious, but it is required to show no favoritism toward the churches. Thus prayer is not a proper activity of the public school because it is not an *ecclesia*. Even a single dissenter has the right not to be offended, coerced, or intimidated. Likewise, the churches cannot expect the state to help support their schools if, at the same time, they wish to be able to inculcate religious values in their students.

Still it is possible for churches and governments to collaborate in areas of mutual interest: day-care projects, programs for the elderly, low-income housing, etc. Such efforts are legitimate if each agency keeps to its proper sphere, respects the unique role of the other, asks no special favors and offers none.

Church/state relations have a rocky road to travel in this era of encroaching government, with such a disparity between vast public resources and very limited church resources. Churches will need to be wary of their autonomy so that the religious community can make its unique prophetic contribution to the commonwealth.

The Process of Politics: Conviction and Compromise

Religion is the realm of conviction. It deals with ultimate reality and with moral purpose, a view of life that sees the good and calls it into being. By contrast, politics is the realm of compromise in which ultimate purposes clash, interest competes with interest, and conflicting claims are adjusted by a process of give and take.

It is seldom possible to translate moral vision directly into public policy, for not all people share the same vision. Moreover our moral vision is always shaped to some extent by our experience and our interests, even when we are not aware that this is so. Thus when we set out to persuade others of the rightness of our cause, we discover that we have to take their visions and interests into account if we are to achieve our objectives. Even then we can only hope to achieve partial success, for our projects always seem to get revised and qualified in the process of getting accepted.

Religious people sometimes find this reality hard to take. They are often contemptuous of politicians who yield to pressure and compromise their ideals. "You should stand up for what you believe is right," they maintain, "even if you go down to defeat in the process."

Should you? Most of the time, our fundamental beliefs are not at stake. The issue is usually a concrete proposal: a law, a policy, a treaty. Even though you support it because you believe in it, part of you knows that the world will not end if you lose. Besides, it may be better to give in a little and survive so you can fight another day.

A good illustration of this process is the ongoing debate about environmental controls. A Clean Air Act sets standards for air quality which factories must meet. Many claim that the cost of meeting those standards is so high that business will suffer. They want the standards lower. Others refute their arguments, calling the economic costs bearable and necessary to maintain the quality of life.

Both groups argue their case, spend money to publicize their cause, bring pressure on lawmakers. What is the politician to do? Past experience suggests that the politician will make some sort of compromise that recognizes the claims of both sides without satisfying either one. The moralist in either camp may protest that the politician has sold out to the other side. The politician in either camp will probably reflect that something was achieved, even if not everything they wanted. Another time, perhaps, they will fare better. That's politics.

The energy for politics comes from interest and conviction. Some pressure groups exist to further the economic or social interests of their supporters. Thus the gun lobby is financed largely by gun manufacturers and hunters. Other groups are founded on moral convictions about an issue. Abortion has called forth both a right-to-life lobby and an abortion rights lobby. These pressure groups keep the politicians, the lawmakers, and even the parties themselves alert to issues they must address.

We have seen, in recent years, a sharp rise in one-issue movements, modeled after the civil rights and peace movements of an earlier decade. They can generate major changes in public policy because they target their efforts, making life unbearable for legislators who are reluctant to go along with them. Their chief value is that they facilitate participation in political activity by ordinary people. They keep politics attuned to people's real concerns, both economic and moral.

The hazard of such groups is that they substitute their own issue for the public good. Many a sensitive and competent lawmaker has been defeated by such groups because they took the wrong stand on the single issue dear to the heart of the pressure group. The intensity of such groups threatens the atmosphere of civility that binds together the body politic. Willfulness, acrimony, and bad temper contaminate the political arena, which requires a certain polite restraint in order to function.

This attitude is especially dangerous when the cause is perceived as a righteous one, for then the antagonist is presumed to be not only wrong but evil. The upright defender of a righteous cause can hardly do business with a wicked enemy, therefore no compromise or accommodation is possible; politics is out of the question.

Such groups are necessary, nonetheless, for if politics is to serve the common good, we need both moral conviction and the spirit of accommodation. We need the hot-eyed partisan and the cool-eyed power broker. Zeal without compromise yields fanaticism, while calculation without conviction yields chicanery. Christians are called to be wise as serpents and innocent as doves, a combination which combines moral passion with a dispassionate adroitness in getting things done.

The People of Politics

Politics is people: people voting for candidates; people running for office; people serving as presidents, governors, mayors, legislators. What kind of people should they be? Is it more important to have people in office who are personally upright, or to have people who are knowledgeable and competent? Should moral or practical considerations prevail in our choice of political leaders?

In addition to moral stature and competence, there is also the matter of how the candidate stands on the issues. We have not gained much if we choose morally upright leaders who are effective in office if their policies are the opposite of what we want to have happen. But there are so many factors to consider, the issues are so complex and unmanageable that many people see competence and morality as better indicators of desirability than the candidate's stand on the issues.

Competence is easiest to assess, at least in theory. A candidate comes before the voting public with a record of performance, but that is not always a reliable guide. Many people—President Truman comes to mind—have had rather lackluster careers until propelled into a demanding office, and only then have they shown their true worth. Others perform well in one capacity only to disappoint when placed in another. Occasionally a young and untried candidate will, upon election, perform with unexpected brilliance. Competence is of admitted importance, but it is not always possible to determine in advance.

Moral considerations are even trickier. Religious considerations can contaminate the political process. We have seen recently a distressing tendency for some people to promote "Christian" candidates whose piety seems to constitute their chief qualification for office. One such candidate stated publicly that he was running because the Lord told him to. The Lord failed to pass his message along to a sufficient number of voters to get the man elected—fortunately.

Church membership or religious commitment is a poor recommendation for public office. It opens up the possibility that politicians may affiliate with a church or experience a religious conversion in order to tap the large, relatively non-political religious constituency. Such an outcome could be disastrous both for our religion and our politics.

Should we oppose a candidate who gambles, runs out on family responsibilities, engages in shady business deals? These are harder questions, but in looking at them we can separate out the public issues from the private.

Biographies of great leaders from other eras have shown us that many a person of great public accomplishments has had a disreputable personal life, degenerate behavior, sex hang-ups and the like. And yet despite all that, they have made major contributions to their society. Today we know far too much about the private lives of public figures and so might well factor out some of what we know—or have been told—when we come to evaluate their public performance. If the quality of their sex life does not affect their public service, then it should not affect our political judgment of them.

Shady business dealings are another matter, because they are likely to affect one's public performance. They raise the question of how far the person can be entrusted with the public business. Does his business life inspire confidence in his personal integrity, his ability to keep promises, his openness about the facts? Is he free of conflicts of interest? Might he get involved in corrupt practices if elected to office?

Corruption is not the only moral issue in public life, but it is an important one. Journalists tend to agree that most office holders are as honest as the rest of us, but they are subject to extreme temptations: campaign contributions, inside tips, stock offers, investment possibilities.

When corrupt practices come to light, some people say, "Well, everybody does it. Why single this person out for punishment?" The answer, of course, is that we can take action only against those cases we know about. Swift and sure reaction by the public is the only way to protect honest politicians from the temptations that go with their vocation.

When corruption is exposed, we should forgive the repentant sinner, while lovingly removing him from office. That action need not be vindictive, but merely the fulfilling of an implicit contract that perhaps voters should make more explicit: "If we catch you with your fingers in the cookie jar, out you go." We cannot discover every wrongdoer, but we can take effective action when one is identified.

Since the corrupt politician may be both competent and effective on the job, some people believe that his faults should be tolerated for the sake of those other qualities. Perhaps that is why the voters so often return to office an incumbent who has been convicted of corrupt practices. But in a democracy no one is indispensable, though many of our senior incumbents seem to feel that they are. If enough conniving politicians are voted into early retirement, others may get the message and find ways to resist the temptations of their office.

The evil of corruption goes beyond favors dispensed or money stolen. The real moral issue is the betrayal of the public trust, the exploitation of the people who are to be served, the contamination of the body politic.

There is a legitimate concern for the quality of moral vision and personal integrity of candidates for public office. As voters we realize that we cannot keep up with every public issue. We know, too, that complex matters cannot be treated adequately in the adversary situation of a political campaign. We cannot expect candidates to spell out in advance just what they would do about every problem facing the government. We cannot even tell what issues will be critical a year hence.

It is right, then, for us to recognize that we are voting, not for an ideology or a program, but a person. We naturally look for leaders who seem trustworthy and believable. Of course we have to watch out for the media-marketed candidate who makes a good appearance before the TV camera. We have to be on guard against the candidate who appeals for our trust without having given any indication of earning it.

But trust is important because we elect leaders to function on our behalf in an unknown future. We often have to judge them on the basis: Is this the sort of person to whom I would entrust the authority of government? Our answer will always involve some risk, but the responsible voter will always ask the question.

We can lower the risk somewhat by participating in the preelection affairs of our political party to insure that the right kind of candidate will be on the ballot on election day. If we find ourselves forced to choose between a knave and a fool, we will already have lost the battle for responsible government.

The Content of Politics: Public Policy

Public policy is what the people decide they want their government to do or not do. It is difficult to talk about "Christian" public policy because there is no one Christian way to run a country. There is no political program which all the faithful ought to support. Nor should there be "Christian political parties," though such things do exist in some countries. Christians can be found on nearly all sides of every significant political issue.

There are, however, some Christian presumptions concerning public policy. They would include a concern for social justice; a bias in favor of the poor, the oppressed, the outsider; a commitment to the solidarity of the whole human family; an investment in the freedom of individuals to develop their own gifts and interests; and a commitment to equal treatment under the law.

These presumptions may imply public policies of a particular sort, but they do not lead us to any exclusive commitment to particular laws or programs. They are more useful in helping us judge existing or proposed policies than in generating them.

LAW AND MORALITY

Christians have long had a tendency to use the law to enforce their own moral commitments. Of course, the law always enforces some version of morality, but its proper function is to regulate conduct that might be harmful to others. The law defends citizens against violence and exploitation. It should not be used to enforce religious obligations, nor should it intrude into private behavior.

Sunday closing laws, which still exist in a few places, are remnants of an attempt to use the law to enforce church discipline, even on those who are not Christians. Certainly everyone is entitled to a day of rest regardless of their religion, but there is no warrant for making the Christian Lord's Day a prescribed day of rest. The increasing pluralism of our society has made this contradiction evident and those laws are rapidly being repealed.

Laws forbidding fornication, adultery, and homosexual activities represent efforts to legislate standards of behavior best left to the judgment of the individual. Except where the public welfare is involved, as in the case of protecting children from sexual exploitation, sexual contacts between consenting adults should not be regulated by law.

It is not always easy to draw the line between personal morality, which should be left up to the individual, and concern for the public interest, which is properly a matter of public policy. In our discussion of abortion, we saw that people differ sharply over what the role of the law should be. Where the views of different sectors of the public differ so dramatically, public policy can emerge only from the inter-play of groups committed to these views, after struggle, com-promise, and accommodation, in which no single view is likely to prevail.

THE WELFARE STATE

The welfare state, perhaps the central and most controver-sial phenomenon of our era, affords an illustration of how our Christian presumptions can help us to evaluate public policy and how differences yet remain after the policy has been es-tablished.

In its simplest form the welfare state consists of that cluster of government programs that provide, through tax reve-nues, for insurance or relief for the aged, the unemployed, the poor, the sick, and the handicapped. It represents society's response to the realities of modern urban-industrial life. It can be seen as an expression of concern for neighbor in need, a concern that lies at the heart of the Christian idea of social justice.

We have seen how the growth in the size and complexity of business and industry necessitated various forms of govern-ment intervention for the protection of the public. The corre-sponding growth of urban-industrial society created a sim-ilar need to provide economic security for an increasingly vulnerable working class—and for a middle class as well.

In an agricultural economy, people might be desperately poor, but most of the time there is enough work to do. The very old and the very sick could be maintained by the family.

A large urban population of industrial workers could not make similar provisions. Cyclical unemployment left whole families without resources. Crowded conditions left no room for old people, who never could earn enough to save up for their old age. Though people tended to live longer, there was no extended family to provide for them.

A corporate response to these conditions was clearly demanded. Every industrial nation has made that response in one way or another. America, with its tradition of individ-ualism, was relatively slow to respond, but finally did so, particularly under the pressure of the great depression.

The first American move toward the welfare state was the development of universal free public education in the nineteenth century. Relief for the poor was initiated by the several states, but those systems broke down under the impact of massive unemployment in the early 1930s. The federal government then responded with old age and survivors' insurance, disability insurance, unemployment insurance, and various welfare programs providing aid for the disabled, the blind, and dependent children.

These vast and far-reaching programs required a similar change in our values and attitudes. We had placed a high premium on self-reliance. We had believed that people ought to save up for their old age. We had viewed public relief as degrading. Our traditional values seemed to be contradicted by the coming of the welfare state.

But our Christian presumptions about public policy offer a basis for affirming the welfare state, and for criticizing it at the same time. It does represent a conscientious effort to witness to the solidarity of the human family. It recognizes our interdependence, our responsibility to and for each other, especially to those most in need. A guarantee of some modest degree of economic security for all is not a matter of charity but of simple justice.

We can see the legitimacy of the system when it offers benefits to us and to our families. Few Americans today, for example, want to abandon the social security program, because they have built it into their own retirement plans, unless they are unusually wealthy. Unemployment compensation and welfare programs are more controversial because they benefit fewer people. Only when one is unemployed does the value of unemployment compensation become clear. It is easy for those who are certain that they will never be "on welfare" to condemn that program for undermining individual initiative.

Even if we accept the legitimacy of this network of social welfare and economic security programs, major problems remain. Most people agree that the social security program needs significant improvement. The condition of the elderly in our society is still not good. The welfare system does, indeed, stifle initiative. And certainly such large, complex, and costly government programs need constant surveillance to insure that waste and abuse are kept to a minimum.

The growing edge of the welfare state is in the area of health care. So far, government activity in this field has been restricted to Medicare and Medicaid, which provide health care for the elderly and the poor. But politicians are now debating whether to extend health care into a full-blown national health insurance program which would include nearly everyone within its purview. What might be a responsible Christian view of this development?

In principle there is little objection to the view that a humane society will do what it can to insure the best possible health care for all. But there the consensus ends. Is this a proper function of government, or should medical care continue to be a private matter? If there is to be a government program, what should be its scope? What provisions would be necessary to keep costs from skyrocketing out of sight? Our earlier discussion of health care suggests that perhaps we ought to make significant changes in the way we use medical care before asking government to pay the bill for a system badly in need of overhaul.

I have my own views on this matter, just as you do. There is no reason why our views should coincide merely because we share the same moral presumptions about public policy. We could disagree over any of the many variables in the whole policy question. If we are fortunate, however, the nation will reach a consensus about what our policy should be in the matter of health care. If we Christians remain true to our convictions about the need for adequate medical care for all, the final shape of our public policy will at least conform to our Christian presuppositions.

Not all Christians approve of the welfare state. Many are opposed to what they regard as the excessive intrusion of government into our lives and the politicization of areas of life that can be better handled in nonpolitical ways. Some feel that the welfare state has made government too large and too remote from the concerns of ordinary people, that we are being smothered by a massive, unresponsive, and expensive bureaucracy. Others are concerned about the paternalistic quality of many government programs which combine to create a new class of clients, increasingly dependent and unable to care for themselves.

These concerns are real and valid. But in giving voice to them, we must also be careful that those of us who are comparatively well off do not begrudge those of us who are less fortunate the help that only government is able to provide. Nor should we resent the use of our tax dollars to provide the help that is given, not in the name of charity but in the name of justice.

The Extension of Politics: Global Community

The twentieth century has seen a vast explosion of transportation and communication that has made us all manifestly citizens of one world community. We need to raise the level of our political consciousness so that we can see all political affairs in their true global perspective, in conformity with the Christian vision of the solidarity of the whole human family. Christians have always believed that all people are the children of God, equally beloved by him, that Christ died for all. We now have the opportunity, indeed we are required, to bring all people into our concern for justice, freedom, and peace.

The nation-state remains a problematical element in world politics. Historians agree that nationalism is by far the most powerful ideology of our century, a fact which came as a surprise to most observers of the world scene. Nationalism is not by any means an unmitigated evil. It has raised people above provincial and tribal loyalties, and that is no small achievement.

That process, however, is still not complete. A generation ago Reinhold Niebuhr noted that the modern state has succeeded in providing internal order and stability, but the international scene is still one of anarchy and disorder. Today even that achievement is in jeopardy, as many nations are torn apart by internal dissension and disorder. In the developing world especially, nation building is a slow and painful process, taking place over the opposition of traditional tribal, ethnic, and religious loyalties.

Still the nation-state continues to be the fundamental unit of the world political order. That fact raises many troubling issues, of which we will look at three that seem predominant: interference in the affairs of other nations; the international economic order; and of course, the overriding issue of peace and war.

OPPRESSION IN OTHER NATIONS

What should be our attitude toward a government that oppresses its own people, jails political opponents without trial, tortures prisoners, and otherwise violates basic human rights? This issue presents us with a genuine dilemma. On the one hand we want to oppose oppression wherever it occurs, and on the other hand we would respect the independence and self-determination of other peoples. How are we to decide which value should prevail?

As we consider this issue, we need to be aware that our own government is not entirely innocent of similar behavior. We have heard revelations concerning the imprisonment of civil rights activists, the harassment of dissenters, the compilation of lists of political enemies, and the systematic cover-up of these activities. Our concern for political oppression in other nations needs to be tempered by humility, for we do not speak from a position of moral superiority.

Our government's official concern about political oppression is complicated by the fact that officials may believe that we need the continuing friendship—or at least the support—of the offending nation. It may occupy a strategically important place in our defense plans. It may be a major supplier of important raw materials.

A further complication is the interaction of these issues with our own domestic politics. Conservatives, for example, single out communist countries for criticism, while liberals condemn right-wing authoritarian governments, though oppression may take similar forms in either case.

Sometimes we make unrealistic demands on other countries to conform to standards of civil liberty that are simply not appropriate to their situation. A nation under siege, or one threatened by terrorism, is likely to take a dim view of civil liberties. Some nations are ruled by authoritarian governments because it is felt that their people are not ready for or do not want democratic rule. We should be cautious about making moralistic judgments in these situations.

But this is not to condone violence, torture, or oppression, all of which are widespread and even perhaps growing in today's world. Can we do anything about it? Sometimes we can. We can work for economic boycotts in an effort to put pressure on oppressive regimes, as was done in the case of Idi Amin's Uganda. Our government can suspend foreign aid or military assistance, as we did in the case of Turkey. We can intervene on behalf of the oppressed with the government itself, as we have done in the case of Soviet Jews. We can at least forego those actions—often unknown to the public—that give aid and comfort to an oppressor, as in the case of Chile.

When such actions are open to us, either as individuals or as a nation, we need to make realistic assessments of the likely results. Will a boycott aid the oppressed or will it make their condition worse? If we discourage business from investing in South Africa, will it pressure the government to abandon its apartheid policy, or will it undercut the economic gains of black people? One's view of the appropriateness of the action will no doubt be shaped by one's reading of the facts of the matter.

The saddest truth is that in many situations we can do little or nothing. Ironically, we can do the most to influence the policies of our allies, but very little to influence adversary nations. We have more influence in Argentina, for example, than in Cambodia. Even where we have little influence, we can make our voices heard in such forums as the United Nations, so that the cause of the oppressed is kept before the eyes of the world.

Our government often has to associate with governments whose oppressive policies we condemn. We cannot afford, for example, to break off negotiations on arms control with the

Soviet Union because of their oppression of Jews and dissidents. These negotiations may ultimately benefit even the oppressed, so they cannot be sacrificed in an attempt to make a dramatic symbolic gesture.

Symbols seldom help the oppressed. Pressure may help. But at the very least our government needs to maintain a persistent concern for those who live under oppression so that in our formation of foreign policy, we do not simply ignore their plight.

THE WORLD ECONOMIC ORDER

Our global consciousness must ultimately extend to the economic realm as well as the political, for our own welfare is linked to the activity of American business as well as our government throughout the world. Observers have often noted that internal conflict and international disputes have been most frequent in the less developed areas of the world. It is easy to see why this is so. Poverty engenders hopelessness and desperation. The poorest people in the world have little to lose by resorting to violence. Every year sees them slipping further behind the developed industrial nations, as the gap widens between the rich nations and the poor.

We need to know more about these conditions because we share some responsibility for them. We have offered only minimal economic assistance to the developing nations, nothing like the generous Marshall Plan that helped to reconstruct Europe after World War II. We have been more interested in selling them arms than in offering them help that would enable them to improve their own economic condition. For most of us, the developing nations are out of sight and out of mind.

Moreover, our own economic activity affects these societies adversely, for our prosperity rests upon their poverty. We thrive because they continue to supply us with cheap raw materials. We have all felt the enormous disruption of the American economy which followed the decision of the OPEC nations to raise the price of crude oil. Only then did we realize that oil had been unnaturally cheap and plentiful up to that moment.

If other developing nations could secure fair prices for their raw materials—such as tin and copper—our own economic prosperity would suffer. We might wonder how long we can sustain our prosperity in the face of this global poverty if we truly believe in the solidarity of the whole human family.

The 1978 Lambeth Conference addressed this issue when it called upon leaders and governments of the world

> . . . to participate actively in the establishment of a new economic order aimed at securing fair prices for raw materials, maintaining fair prices for manufactured goods, and reversing the process by which the rich become richer and the poor poorer.[3]

The bishops recognized that to take this demand seriously would require those of us who live in the developed industrial nations to "face the necessity of a redistribution of wealth and trading opportunities."[4] If such a change in the world economic scene were to take place, we might find our own prosperity threatened. Our concern for social justice and the solidarity of the human family should lead us to pay that price, not only willingly but gladly.

Individual Christians may not be able to do much to change the nature of the world economy, but we can make the effort to take a serious look at how the system works so that we can exercise some moral responsibility for changing it in the direction of greater fairness and equity. An informed and enlightened public opinion can have a significant effect on the way we do business in the rest of the world.

PEACE AND WAR

International conflict is the most dramatic and frightening threat to the future of mankind. The existence of intercontinental ballistics missiles equipped with multiple nuclear warheads poses an almost incomprehensible danger of mass destruction and death. What creative possibilities can the Christian community see in this tragic situation?

The Christian presumption is in favor of peace; the burden of proof rests with those who would justify any decision to go to war. Moreover, a Christian analysis would require that the decision for war be made only as a last resort, and after all efforts at negotiation in good faith have failed. Once the decision is made, moral obligations do not cease, for war itself should be fought within limits, for limited goals, and with all possible restraint.

There is thus no moral justification for the carpet-bombing of defenseless civilians, for wholesale destruction of cities, for slaughter of prisoners or those suspected of collaborating with the enemy. The twentieth-century concept of total war, in which anything is allowable, is not compatible with the Christian conscience. Nor is the concept of "unconditional surrender," which caused so much unnecessary death and destruction in our war with Japan.

There is, of course, a view long expressed in the Christian community that war in any form is unthinkable; that no Christian can ever participate in any war. Pacifism is not a new phenomenon; it was the universally held position of the primitive church. When Christ told Peter to sheathe his sword (Mt. 26:52) he repudiated violence on the part of his followers, it was believed. Therefore, no Christian should ever bear the sword.

Modern pacifists add the practical argument that wars are usually fought, not as a last resort but in pursuit of aims which are illegitimate in themselves. They add that, no matter how frightful are the conditions that lead to war, they are better than the conditions created by war. War never solves problems; it creates them. The human costs inevitably outweigh any good that might be achieved by war. The Christian, therefore, should always be prepared to suffer violence, but steadfastly refuse to perpetrate it.

This position is not accepted by most Christians today, but it is represented in every Christian body. It is a valid Christian response to the question of war and should be respected even when it is not affirmed. The moral weight of the pacifist position can help Christians to avoid the temptation to opt for war casually or enthusiastically, with a self-righteous fervor that justifies any atrocity on our side, while assuming the enemy to be somewhat less than human.

The most serious issue today is not pacifism but the easy

assumption that war is necessary and/or inevitable. Christians cannot responsibly accept either assertion. Our moral commitment places us on the side of the peacemakers, who refuse to accept the inevitability of armed conflict.

REVOLUTION

Just as significant as war is the issue of revolution in the modern world, for revolutions are just as violent as wars and sometimes more so. Yet we must recognize that in some circumstances, oppression may be so unbearable and alternatives so scarce that violent revolution may be the only responsible choice before a people.

Americans should be able to understand that because our own nation was founded in revolution. Christians should understand it too, because the church has long held a doctrine of justifiable revolution, stemming from both Catholic and Calvinist sources.

Some Christians tend to sentimentalize revolution as a solution to the problem of injustice and oppression. It is easy to ignore the fact that many revolutionary groups are just as violent and oppressive as the regimes they seek to replace. Oppression "in the name of the people" is not morally superior to oppression "of the people," as many of the people discovered, often too late.

The Christian moral presumption favors civil order, just as it favors peace. Like war, revolution may be justified as a last resort, but only as a last resort. Before supporting a violent revolution, the Christian needs to assess the possibility that the violence engendered will truly produce a situation that is so beneficial that the suffering will be worthwhile. Our historical experience with violent revolution does not offer much hope that this will be the case.

THE ARMS RACE:
CONVENTIONAL AND NUCLEAR WEAPONS

In the matter of armed conflict, our generation has been faced with a new dilemma created by the existence of nuclear armaments. It was bad enough when the United States and Russia faced each other like two scorpions in a bottle, as the saying went. But the threat of mutual annihilation was so powerful then that, no matter who had how many weapons, thermonuclear war was truly unthinkable.

Today these two nations no longer enjoy a monopoly of nuclear weapons. It may, indeed, be possible for any nation, no matter how small, to develop an atomic or hydrogen bomb. Even nameless terrorist groups may be able to manufacture such a bomb and use it for a form of nuclear blackmail. The first priority for world peace, therefore, must be a serious commitment to reduce and control nuclear armaments.

Even aside from nuclear weapons, we are witnessing a worldwide arms race unparalleled in human history. Our own arms sales to the rest of the world have constituted a major contribution to that race. American arms have escalated the level of violence in conflicts all over the world. We have witnessed wars in which each side used American-supplied arms against the other.

Those arms sales represent large profits for American manufacturers, large expenditures by our government, and large additions to the value of our exports, favorably affecting our balance of payments. Yet we have to accept the moral responsibility for increasing the level of armed violence throughout the world. If there is any cause on which peace-loving people can unite, it surely must be the reduction of our unhappy role as arms merchants for the world.

The worldwide arms race raises similar questions about our own national defense posture, which has been a major source of controversy since the beginning of the cold war. Certainly no reasonable person can deny the necessity for a strong national defense. Surely our national security is a valid political goal. The difficulty comes when we begin to ask, "What is an adequate national defense?"

Too often the question is answered in terms that suggest that if we do not spend the additional dollar—or billion dollars—then we are threatened with immediate annihilation. As a result, no patriotic legislator feels it politically safe to question any defense expenditure.

The consequences have been predictable. Somehow we never seem to have enough defense. Though we have spent trillions of dollars on defense since World War II, there are further trillions in plans on the drawing board and in Department of Defense proposals.

At the same time, weaponry has become so sophisticated that it becomes obsolete before it goes into production. Many complicated new weapons systems never perform as promised. And they all seem to cost far more than anticipated, as multibillion-dollar cost overruns are commonplace. Political pressure from defense-related industries and labor unions makes it unlikely that defense costs will ever be brought under control.

This attitude toward national defense is based on highly questionable presuppositions: the fear of death and the illusion that money can buy total security. People who are terrified of the possibility of death will cling to life for all they are worth. Just as some people will justify any medical procedure that promises to prolong life at whatever cost, so they will justify any defense program at whatever expense because of the hope, however faint, that this weapons system will finally put us ahead of the Russians. And if we don't spend the money, they'll catch up with us and then it will be all over.

But in point of fact, any Christian knows that we cannot buy total security here on earth. Life is risky at best and we are called to face it with faith and courage. We cannot place our ultimate trust in weapons systems because they will ultimately fail us, no matter how much we may have paid for them.

In our dealings with our international adversaries, our best recourse is to rely on negotiation, accommodation, and compromise, as we do in domestic politics. We will not always get our way, but the experience of the past thirty years suggests that reliance on armaments creates as many problems for us as it solves.

This is not to say that we do not need armed strength. But it does suggest that there are limits beyond which more armaments do not contribute to our true national security. We are still by far the most powerful nation on the face of the earth, perhaps more powerful than we need to be. In the days to come, we will find that power to be ever more irrelevant to the issues we face and the decisions we are called to make on the international scene.

The World Christian Network

Christians have some unique resources for our reflections upon and our response to global issues. The Church of Christ is a universal body. As Christians we are citizens of the world; we are members of an international community. We maintain relationships with other Christians in all the nations of the earth.

Those relationships are more than theoretical. Through such entities as the Anglican Communion and the World Council of Churches, we are brought into face-to-face contact with Christian leaders throughout the world. We have sources of information independent of governments and the secular press. We can often find out with greater accuracy just what is going on in certain countries, what is the state of the lives of ordinary people there. We can get a look at their problems from their own perspective.

Literature is available to us from international agencies and from the churches of other countries. Visiting church leaders can tell their stories in person, even in remote corners of the nation. Many Americans make contact with local church groups when they travel abroad.

These linkages can help us to make intelligent responses to conditions in other nations. They can help us to influence the foreign policy of our own government, by sharing information which our own officials may not have. We can encourage public officials to respond to situations where they might not otherwise see that we have some legitimate concern.

Foreign policy is not a matter confined exclusively to senior statesmen and career diplomats; it involves every citizen, and ordinary Christians can make a creative contribution to it. As long as we believe in a universal church with a worldwide mission, we will be concerned with what is happening on the international scene and will do what we can, however modestly, to influence that scene.

WHAT CAN A CHRISTIAN DO?

Even this cursory examination of political issues demonstrates the enormous range and complexity of contemporary political life. How can an ordinary Christian exercise any leverage on this incredibly complicated enterprise? Most of us feel quite powerless to affect the political system, no matter how knowledgeable we are. What can ordinary people do?

The issue is an important one because political participation is part of our Christian duty. In biblical times, it was enough for the ordinary subject to be obedient, as both Paul and Peter admonished. Government was in the hands of rulers and one's duty was simply to obey. But in a democracy we are all called to be rulers. Our Christian duty involves us, not just in obeying the laws but in active participation in the processes that make laws and public policy. How can that responsibility be exercised?

First we can affirm the political vocation. Some Christians should go into politics if they are competent and sensitive to the issues, if they care about people and are effective in political work. Others should work in public service occupations where they can contribute to the common good. Too long have religious people regarded politics as dirty business, fit only for the corrupt. We have to abandon that heresy and encourage conscientious Christians to get into the act.

Some will do that professionally. Others will do it as volunteers in political campaigns, as neighborhood workers, as activists in issue-oriented organizations. The religious community should encourage their activities and give them opportunities to share their experiences.

The local church can provide a forum for raising our global consciousness. Concern for the world mission of the church should be a part of every parish educational program. We need to go beyond church affairs, however, and learn something of the political and economic context in which that mission takes place. Then we can begin to make the connections between what we have learned and what our country's policies are doing to other nations.

Christians, singly or together, can mount an informed critique of public policy, foreign and domestic. We can discuss political issues within a theological framework, identifying our Christian presumptions and testing various policies in their light. We cannot deal with everything, but we can deal with some things. Dealing with even one thing will put us ahead of most people.

Even those of us who are not politically active can be a part of an enlightened public opinion. We can do more than just reflect the findings of the latest public opinion poll. We can form our own opinions and express them when we get the chance.

We can occasionally let our elected representatives know what we think about a particular issue, especially when we suspect that our view may run counter to the main stream of opinion. Suppose thousands of Christians were to let their congressmen know that they are willing to tolerate higher taxes in the interest of providing adequate public services to all, especially the poor. That might effect a political revolution.

But some people are naturally nonpolitical. They may resonate to the arts, perhaps, rather than politics, and define the good life in aesthetic rather than political terms. That, too, is a legitimate Christian response. There is no disgrace in being nonpolitical.

But in a democracy, even the most nonpolitical types are obligated to participate at least minimally in public life. They ought to vote. They ought to know, when election day comes, where the polling place is located and who is running for what. They should follow the campaigns at least closely enough so that they can vote with reasonable intelligence. Total apathy is a disease that responsible Christians must cast off. Our participation in the political process is our personal contribution to justice and peace in the social order.

· 13 ·

——

The Church
and the Moral Life

——

Most of the discussion in this book has focused on the moral life of the individual. We have considered the development of moral character, how decisions are made, and what kinds of issues face us in personal and family life as well as on the larger social, economic, and political scene. How shall I live? What shall I do? have been our primary concerns.

This approach would seem to assume that our moral life is lived out in isolation. But that can be only part of the story, for Christianity is a venture in community. The Christian faith is a common possession of the people of God, the company of faithful people who gather for prayer and worship, fellowship and service. No consideration of the Christian life would be complete without putting it into the context of community: the church.

Anglicans have always taken the church very seriously, regarding it as more than an aggregate of individual believers. In the creed we confess our faith in the one, holy, catholic, and apostolic church, the universal body of Christian believers down through the ages. The church is the divine society called into being by God, in which Christ is encountered in word and sacrament, in which we are empowered by the indwelling Holy Spirit. To be a Christian is to be a member of the church, a living part of a living body.

The church appears in history in many forms. The religious organization, the denomination, is the church—the Protestant Episcopal Church in the United States of America, for example, with its constitution and canons, its officials and assemblies and stated positions. The local congregation is the church, perhaps the most influential form of the church for the life of the ordinary Christian.

But the church is also those less formal associations of Christians who come together outside the official structures of the church. "Where two or three are gathered in my name," Jesus said, "there am I in the midst of them" (Mt. 18:20). The Christian family is one of these assemblies of the faithful. A neighborhood group might be one too, or a prayer group on the job, an informal group of friends, a church-related interest group. All of these communities partake of the character of the church, and in all of these settings the church has some impact on the moral life of the Christian.

The Church and Moral Formation

We noted at the outset that this book is intended to be helpful to people of faith who are committed to Christ and who care about doing the Lord's will in their lives. They need help in learning how to work out the implications of their faith, figuring out what they ought to do and how they ought to do it. In other words, we presume the existence of the committed Christian moral agent.

Where do such persons come from? Not everyone shares this commitment and concern for doing the Lord's will. Even many Christians have a very restricted view of their own moral responsibilities. How are serious, ethically sensitive Christians produced?

Such people are the product of a long process of nurture. They have been shaped by their environment, which has enabled them to become morally sensitive and concerned. For the Christian, that environment is the community of faith, the church.

The family is, of course, the most important agency in the moral development of the child. Children pick up the faith of their parents, their convictions, their attitudes, their moral commitments. Often the process is unconscious. The children may be well along into adulthood before they realize that they are living out moral commitments quite similar to those of their parents.

But that process is neither simple nor certain, for we live in a world in which the family is under severe stress, as we have already seen. Other agencies in the society offer moral alternatives. Conflicting values are aggressively promoted. Acquisitiveness, competitiveness, and sheer selfishness are promoted all around us.

The perils of competing value systems require the Christian family to be more self-conscious and intentional about the moral formation of children. Parents need to be able to identify their own convictions and to speak freely about them. They need to share with their children their perception that something important is at stake in the preservation of their values. Parents need to be able to offer convincing reasons for their own moral choices so that children will understand what those values mean to them.

Beyond the work of the family itself, the local church can affirm and support this process of moral formation. It should be a major ingredient in the parish education program. While parents cannot expect the parish to do all their own work of moral instruction, in a time when even the most thoughtful parents feel inadequate to the task, the whole Christian community needs to learn to share that responsibility.

A more subtle but no less important instrument for moral development is the worship of the church. Regular participation in the hearing of the Word and reception of the sacrament contributes to moral formation. Even when ethical issues are not directly addressed, in worship we meet a Lord who loves us and who calls us out of our preoccupation with self. In worship we identify and acknowledge our moral failures, we offer up our moral dilemmas, we receive forgiveness of our sins and offenses. In worship we hear the call to share God's love with all of his children and are sent forth to serve in the cause of freedom, justice, and peace. Worship creates a context that contrasts sharply with the aggressive, competitive, and self-centered ethos of contemporary society.

Moral formation is not a matter that concerns only children, for all of us are in the process of moral development. We all need constant feeding and nurture. We need to have heightened our awareness of the issues to which the Gospel speaks. Getting our consciousness raised may take some effort, especially where our self-interest is involved and where it is profitable for us not to raise moral questions.

It may be easy for me to see, for example, that the youth of the community are having problems with drugs. It may be harder for me to see that my own use of pills or alcohol may contribute to the climate that makes drugs a problem for others. The church can help me look for the links between these issues so that I become aware of the extent to which I share responsibility for someone else's moral quandary.

We have seen how the operations of business, labor, government, and various professional groups all raise significant moral issues. Many of the major decision-makers in these areas are members of local churches. Many of them would concede that their church has never provided them with any guidance or support in their public role. Indeed the church seems to have little interest in such matters. A responsible effort at moral formation would include such people within its compass to help insure that Christians in all sorts of occupations may become effective and responsible moral agents.

A parish might make use of Lawrence Kohlberg's analysis of the process of moral development as an instrument in building a program of moral formation. His conceptual model helps us to understand how we are led from one level of development to the next. It can suggest ways to teach—and ways not to teach—helping us to become more conscious of the effects of our behavior on the moral development of Christians, both youth and adults.

Kohlberg helps us to understand the power of socializing forces among teen-agers. Instead of inveighing against the demonic influence of peer-group pressures, for example, we might become more self-conscious about creating supportive peer groups, as many churches have done, often quite unconsciously. We can help adults to move beyond the moralistic law-and-order stage, in which so many Americans seem to be stuck, by affirming the centrality of unbounded love in the Christian life.

Kohlberg's theory is not the only conceptual scheme available for moral development, to be sure. Whatever the theory, the important thing is to see the church as a major contributor to the development of responsible moral agents. When Christians can see the connections between their faith and their behavior, between their religious convictions and the great moral issues of the day, then the church has indeed fulfilled this most significant aspect of its mission.

A Community of Moral Discourse

Christians need the opportunity to talk about specific ethical issues. Many of those issues are so complex that a simple acquaintance with the facts is difficult to achieve. But we need to know the facts before we can make responsible judgments. We need to be able to discuss those facts and our responses to them, in a climate that is free of self-serving propaganda.

Many of those issues are bitterly controversial. We need to be able to talk about them in a context where opposing voices can be heard without lapsing into shrill and vicious name-calling. We need to be able to speak and hear the truth in a context of love and mutual support and concern. Only in such a context can faithful Christians thoughtfully relate the facts of the case to their religious convictions and then go on to make responsible actions.

A Christian congregation can provide a forum where ethical issues can be aired. We can look together at such controversial matters as drug abuse, abortion, homosexuality, child rearing, in an atmosphere characterized by a Christian concern for justice, truth, and love, and free from the rancor and deliberate falsification that cloud so much of our public discussion about controversial issues.

In the fellowship of the Christian community, we can begin to look at the concrete moral choices faced by actual people, bringing our ethical discourse out of the realm of abstraction. People who trust and care for each other can even begin to share their own moral experience, referring their concerns and dilemmas to the thoughtful consideration of their fellow Christians.

Many parishes are reluctant to see the congregation engage in such discussions, precisely because the issues are likely to be controversial. Many churches are simply afraid of conflict. They believe that Christians should always be nice to each other. The introduction of controversy makes it hard to be nice, so we should deal only with things we all agree about.

That is a very limited view of Christian community. If the common faith and mutual love which binds the congregation together does not enable its members to engage in responsible discourse on matters that deeply concern them, then where is such interchange ever to take place? Speaking the truth in love requires both restraint and a willingness to take risks. A morally committed church will be able to provide the context in which moral discourse can flourish without being destroyed in the process.

Valuable work of moral reflection can be carried on by intentional groups of people who band together to study and act upon some issue which they all regard as important. Some such groups have formal organizational structure: The Episcopal Peace Fellowship, Integrity, The Church and City Conference, the Church and Society Network.

Such groups are able to gather information about their area of interest, consult with knowledgeable people in the field, call on sympathetic theologians and ethical thinkers, publish and disseminate the results of their reflections. They may engage in action projects to bring about the results they advocate. Groups such as these can be expected to do most of the spade work of ethical reflection on particular personal and social issues on behalf of the larger church.

The Church as Moral Model

The church influences the world as much by what it is and does as by what it says. The moral life of the Christian community carries a message to the world, whether we intend it or not.

Too often the church teaches all the wrong things. When a parish plays the "Get the Rector" game, or when a power struggle in the congregation sets people against each other, when conflict becomes mean and spiteful or petty and meaningless, then the world sees the church denying by its life the truth which it proclaims. Thus the Christian community stands under the demand of its Lord to live out its own life with integrity and sensitivity, furthering the cause of justice and love in its own corporate life.

This demand applies not only to the interpersonal relationships within congregations, but to the institutional behavior of the church as well. It may be noble for the church to fight to raise the minimum wage, but its witness is subverted if that same church underpays its own employees. Churches have a generally poor reputation for their personnel policies, especially regarding lay employees: secretaries, sextons, etc. The pay is generally poor; there is little job security; most employees lack adequate pension plans. On the whole, churches are not good employers, a fact which the outside world knows quite well.

The church can best teach its values by exemplifying them. The witness of the historic peace churches, the Friends, Mennonites, Brethren, shows how powerful can be the effect of such acted-out commitment. Pacifism has been part of their corporate discipline for many years. Despite their small size, those churches have been quite influential in establishing the legitimacy of conscientious objection to war and in bringing the cause of peace constantly before the general public.

Because of its diversity and its legacy of commitment to personal freedom, the Episcopal Church has never been strong in the area of church discipline. Indeed it has almost seemed to some outsiders to have proclaimed a doctrine of moral laxity. Within the broad range of that freedom available within the church, particular congregations and other groups can frame a corporate discipline for acting out their moral convictions in specific ways. If we are to repudiate the cultural value of acquisitiveness, for example, we must discover ways to demonstrate that repudiation by the quality of our corporate lives.

Similarly, the church has repeatedly asserted its commitment to the city, especially to the poor and the other victims of urban blight and decay. Those proclamations will enjoy credibility only as the church engages in significant corporate activity consistent with that commitment. It will mean deploying our human and financial resources for the benefit of those who suffer exploitation and oppression in the city. That kind of advocacy will carry a message more powerful and convincing than any convention resolution or episcopal pronouncement.

Finally the church needs to discover ways in which its own life can testify to its commitment to the solidarity of the whole human family. In this most heterogeneous nation, our local churches normally consist of people who look alike, dress alike, have about the same income, hold similar jobs. There are few multiracial, multiethnic, classless congregations anywhere to be found. Changing this situation will require considerable thought and effort, but it must be achieved if the organized church is to make a credible witness in the midst of the diversity of our society.

The Church as a Community of Support

The moral life is a struggle in which we win some and lose some. The individual can be weighed down by the struggle, overwhelmed with a sense of failure, or, on the other hand, glide blissfully along on a wave of complacency, unaware of any moral lapses or even challenges. For these reasons Christians need to maintain their roots in a caring community of faith and love which can provide both accountability and support.

As we try to live out our moral commitments, we need to let others into our life, to know our concerns and our dilemmas, to help us look at the choices before us, to help us evaluate the choices we have made, to support us when we need courage, and to forgive us when we fail.

Failure is the hardest reality for us to face. We make excuses, blame others, practice denial. That is the nature of sin. But in the knowledge of the love of God, we can afford to face our failures and repudiate our own evil deeds. We can dare to ask forgiveness in the knowledge that we will be forgiven.

The Christian community offers the fellowship in which all this can happen. We can be accepted and affirmed, renewed and strengthened to face another day, another choice, another dilemma—even another failure.

The moral life of the Christian is the most significant aspect of the Christian ministry in the world. That ministry is shared by every Christian and is carried out in every conceivable environment: in the home, on the job, among our friends, in our public roles, and in our private lives. Christian behavior rises to the level of ministry when it becomes a self-conscious response to the call of the Lord who saves us and redeems us.

Many congregations have come to understand the importance of this concept of lay ministry and have encouraged the creation of groups that provide accountability and support for one another. But this is a relatively new phenomenon in the Episcopal Church, for most church members still regard the moral life as strictly private and personal.

The most significant task facing the church in our generation is the mobilizing of our moral energies by bringing the moral life out of the closet and into the mainstream of our corporate life. Only then will we see how it is related to the totality of Christian life: our worship, our spiritual pilgrimage, our various public roles. For no facet of Christian life and thought stands by itself. The recognition of the interrelatedness of all of life—and all of our lives—is the ultimate consequence of the hearing of the Gospel.

Notes

CHAPTER ONE

1. William Wordsworth, "Ode to Duty."
2. Matthew Arnold, "Literature and Dogma."
3. Thomas Paine, *The Rights of Man*.
4. Benjamin Franklin, *Autobiography and Other Writings* (Boston: Houghton-Mifflin Co., 1958), p. 74.
5. Frederick Denison Maurice to Mr. Ludlow, 1853; Quoted in Alec R. Vidler, *Witness to the Light* (New York: Charles Scribner's Sons, 1948), p. 29.
6. Richard Hooker, *Of the Laws of Ecclesiastical Polity*, ed. Georges Edelen (Cambridge: Harvard University Press, Belknap Press, 1977), bk. III, chap. 10.

CHAPTER TWO

1. H. Richard Niebuhr, *The Responsible Self* (New York: Harper & Row, 1963), pp. 47–68.
2. Aristotle, *Ethica Nicomachea*, bk. II, 6, quoted in Ibid., p. 57.
3. Kohlberg outlines these stages in an appendix to an article, "Stages of Moral Development as a Basis for Moral Education," in C. M. Beck, B. S. Crittenden, and E. V. Sullivan, eds., *Moral Education: Interdisciplinary Approaches* (Toronto: University of Toronto, 1971), pp. 86–92. My discussion is based on an excellent summary and analysis of Kohlberg's theory in Ronald Duska and Mariellen Whelan, *Moral Development: A Guide to Piaget and Kohlberg* (New York: Paulist Press, 1975), pp. 42–79.
4. Immanuel Kant, *Critique of Practical Reason*.

CHAPTER THREE

1. Paul Lehmann, *Ethics in a Christian Context* (New York: Harper & Row, 1963), pp. 126–28.

2. Joseph Fletcher, *Situation Ethics: The New Morality* (Philadelphia: Westminster Press, 1966), p. 79.

3. Ibid.

4. See Harvey Cox, ed., *The Situation Ethics Debate* (Philadelphia: Westminster Press, John C. Bennett, et al., *Storm over Ethics* (Philadelphia: United Church Press, 1967).

5. Fletcher, *Situation Ethics*, pp. 64–68.

6. John C. Bennett in *Situation Ethics Debate*, pp. 68–69.

7. Wilford O. Cross in *Situation Ethics Debate*, p. 76; John M. Swomley, p. 90.

8. For a survey of natural law in contemporary Roman Catholic thinking, see Charles E. Curran, "Absolute Norms in Moral Theology," Gene Outka and Paul Ramsey, eds., *Norm and Context in Christian Ethics* (New York: Charles Scribner's Sons, 1968), pp. 139–173.

9. John C. Bennett, *Christian Ethics and Social Policy* (New York: Charles Scribner's Sons, 1946), pp. 120 ff.

10. J. Philip Wogaman, *A Christian Method of Moral Judgment* (Philadelphia: Westminster Press, 1976), pp. 38–48.

11. Ibid., pp. 70–110.

12. James M. Gustafson, "Context Versus Principles: A Misplaced Debate in Christian Ethics," Martin E. Marty and Dean G. Peerman, eds., *New Theology No. 3* (New York: Macmillan Co., 1966), p. 98.

13. Ibid., p. 89.

14. Fletcher, *Situation Ethics*, p. 32.

CHAPTER FOUR

1. Richard Hooker, *Of the Laws of Ecclesiastical Polity*, bk. III, chap. 10.

2. Though I have approached the material differently, I have received much help in this discussion from Bruce C. Birch and Larry L. Rasmussen, *Bible and Ethics in the Christian Life* (Minneapolis: Augsburg Publishing House, 1976), especially chapter 6.

CHAPTER FIVE

1. Tom Wolfe, "The Me Decade and the Third Great Awakening," *Mauve Gloves and Madmen, Clutter & Vine* (New York: Bantam Books, 1977), pp. 111–147.

CHAPTER SIX

1. For this view, I am indebted to Derrick Sherwin Bailey, *Sexual Relation in Christian Thought* (New York: Harper & Bros., 1959), chap. 7; the idea is further developed in Paul K. Jewett, *Man as Male and Female* (Grand Rapids: Wm. B. Eerdmans, 1975).

2. This discussion relies heavily on Bailey, *Sexual Relation,* especially chaps. 3 to 5.

3. John H. Snow illuminates the motives and the hazards involved in contemporary marriage and its alternatives in *On Pilgrimage: Marriage in the Seventies* (New York: Seabury Press, 1971).

4. Arlo Karlen, *Sexuality and Homosexuality* (New York: Norton, 1971) offers a good introduction to the subject as well as fine bibliography.

5. Norman Pittenger, "A Theological Approach to Understanding Homosexuality," in Ruth Tiffany Barnhouse and Urban T. Holmes III, eds., *Male and Female: Christian Approaches to Sexuality* (New York: Seabury Press, 1976), pp. 164–66.

6. C. S. Lewis, *Mere Christianity* (New York: Macmillan Co., 1943), p. 80.

CHAPTER SEVEN

1. Title I Canon 17. Sec. 4(d).

2. Derrick Sherwin Bailey, *Sexual Relation* (New York: Harper and Bros., 1959), pp. 197, 208.

3. *The Lambeth Conference, 1958* (London, S.P.C.K.) Resolution 115.

4. Title I Canon 18. Sec. 2, 3.

5. Robert Farrar Capon, *Bed and Board* (New York: Simon & Schuster, 1965), p. 21.

6. See chap. 2, above.

7. John Snow, *On Pilgrimage: Marriage in the Seventies.*

CHAPTER EIGHT

1. Alfred North Whitehead, *Religion in the Making* (New York: Meridian Books, 1960), p. 16.

2. Quoted in Reinhold Niebuhr, *Moral Man and Immoral Society* (New York: Charles Scribner's Sons, 1941), p. 267.

CHAPTER NINE

1. Gibson F. Winter, *The New Creation as Metropolis* (New York: Macmillan, 1963), pp. 1–6.

CHAPTER TEN

1. Daniel Callahan, *Abortion: Law, Choice and Morality* (New York: Macmillan, 1970). I have relied heavily on Callahan's work in this discussion.

2. *Journal of the General Convention*, 1976, C-1.

CHAPTER TWELVE

1. Thomas Jefferson, "Second Inaugural Address," Henry S. Commager, *Living Ideas in America* (New York: Harper Bros., 1951), p. 149.

2. Reinhold Niebuhr, *The Children of Light and the Children of Darkness* (New York: Charles Scribner's Sons, 1944), xiii.

3. *Report of the Lambeth Conference, 1978* (London: Church Information Center, 1978), p. 35.

4. Ibid., p. 34.

Suggestions
for Further Reading

The reader who is interested in pursuing further any of the issues raised in this book might begin by looking over the works cited in notes to the various chapters. In addition, the following books probe more deeply into areas that I have been able only to touch upon. Most of these works do not require a wide background in the field of ethics in order to be understood. Some of them are relatively old—old enough to offer the perspective of another era, a useful contribution to ethical discussion today.

GENERAL TREATMENTS

During the 1950s a number of books on ethics were published for the benefit of educated lay persons. Among the most enduring of these are Stephen F. Bayne, Jr., *Christian Living* (New York: Seabury, 1957), a part of the original Church's Teaching Series; William A. Spurrier, *Guide to the Good Life* (New York: Charles Scribner's Sons, 1955); James A. Pike, *Doing the Truth* (Garden City, N.Y.: Doubleday, 1955); and Howard Clark Kee, *Making Ethical Decisions* (Philadelphia: Westminster, 1957), a volume in the Layman's Theological Library.

Those interested in pursuing the Anglican position on Christian ethics could begin with Paul Elmer More and Frank Leslie Cross, *Anglicanism* (London: S.P.C.K., 1962), a collection of source material from the seventeenth century Anglican divines. The section on ethics is especially useful. Basil Willey, *The English Moralists* (New York: W. W. Norton, 1964) is not primarily theological in its orientation, but it does convey the range and quality of Anglican thinking. Frank M. McClain, *Maurice: Man and Moralist* (London: S.P.C.K., 1972) offers insight into the thought of Anglicanism's greatest modern theologian. R. C. Mortimer, *Christian Ethics* (London: Hutchinson House, 1950) is an exemplary treatment of the traditional themes of authority and duty as applied to sex, war, gambling, and other issues.

The ethical teaching of the New Testament is treated in John Knox, *The Ethic of Jesus in the Teaching of the Church* (New York: Abingdon, 1961); T. W. Manson, *Ethics and the Gospel* (New York: Charles Scribner's Sons, 1960); Ernest F. Scott, *Man and Society in the New Testament* (New York: Charles Scribner's Sons, 1946); and Amos N. Wilder, *Eschatology and Ethics in the Teaching of Jesus* (New York: Harper and Brothers, 1939).

Stanley Hauerwas has made a major contribution to the ethics of character in *Character and the Christian Life* (San Antonio: Trinity University Press, 1975), an issue which is also treated in James M. Gustafson, *Can Ethics Be Christian?* (Chicago: University of Chicago Press, 1975). A number of Gustafson's more important essays are collected in his *Theology and Christian Ethics* (Philadelphia: Pilgrim Press, 1974). Recent Roman Catholic ethical thinking is summarized in George M. Regan, *New Trends in Moral Theology* (New York: Newman Press, 1971). A perceptive treatment of the relationship between natural law and situational thinking is William A. Spurrier, *Natural Law and the Ethics of Love: A New Synthesis* (Philadelphia: Westminster, 1974).

Issues relating to sexuality and sex roles have spawned a large number of books in recent years. Among the more useful are Kenneth and Alice Hamilton, *To Be a Man, To Be a Woman* (Nashville: Abingdon, 1972), a study book that deals with attitudes and beliefs about sex roles; Anthony Kosnik et al., *Human Sexuality: New Directions in American Catholic Thought* (New York: Paulist, 1977), a symposium initiated by the Catholic Theology Society of America. Charles E. Curran, a major voice in the American Catholic Church offers insight into methods of ethical reflection in *Issues in Sexual and Medical Ethics* (Notre Dame: University of Notre Dame Press, 1978), while James B. Nelson performs a similar task from a Protestant perspective in *Embodiment: An Approach to Sexuality and Christian Theology* (Minneapolis: Augsburg, 1978). Ruth Tiffany Barnhouse discusses homosexuality in *Homosexuality: a Symbolic Confusion* (New York: Seabury, 1977). Marriage and the family are considered in an international perspective in a collection of essays by Roman Catholic scholars in Franz Böckle, ed., *The Future of Marriage as an Institution* (New York: Herder and Herder, 1970). Edward V. Stein, ed., *Fathering: Fact or Fable* (Nashville: Abingdon, 1977) treats fatherhood in the light of contemporary psychology and social change.

William Temple, *Christianity and the Social Order* (New York: Penguin, 1942) is still required reading for anyone who wants to understand the Anglican perspective on society. Gibson Winter, ed., *Social Ethics* (New York: Harper and Row, 1968) assembles the reflections of major ethical thinkers on a number of significant social issues and includes a thoughtful introductory essay by the editor. The work of the church in the social order is described in Gayraud S. Wilmore, *The Secular Relevance of the Church* (Philadelphia: Westminster, 1962), while William Stringfellow offers a critique of contemporary society in *An Ethic for Christians and Others in a Strange Land* (Waco, Texas: Word Books, 1973). Other theological analyses of contemporary society include Gibson Winter, *Being Free* (New York: Macmillan, 1970) and *To Hear and to Heed* (Cincinnati: Forward Movement Publications, 1978), the report of the hearings on urban life conducted by the Urban Bishops' Coalition.

Right use of the physical environment is the subject of Michael P. Hamilton, *This Little Planet* (New York: Charles Scribner's Sons, 1970). Hamilton has also assembled a collection of position papers on genetics and medical research in *The New Genetics and the Future of Man* (Grand Rapids: Wm. B. Eerdmans, 1972), which should be read along with Paul Ramsey, *Fabricated Man: The Ethics of Genetic Control* (New Haven: Yale University Press, 1970). James R. Adams, *The Sting of Death* (New York: Seabury, 1971) is designed for study groups concerned with the way in which Christians face death and bereavement.

Ethical issues in the world of business are treated in a light but serious manner in William A. Spurrier, *Ethics and Business* (New York: Charles Scribner's Sons, 1962). Wilfred Beckerman makes a persuasive case for economic growth on ethical grounds in *Two Cheers for the Affluent Society* (New York: St. Martin's Press, 1974). Norbert Greinacher and Alois Müller, *The Poor and the Church* (New York: Seabury, 1977) is a collection of papers by Roman Catholic scholars which should prove informative for Christians of all persuasions.

Richard John Neuhaus, *Christian Faith and Public Policy* (Minneapolis: Augsburg, 1977) offers a theological perspective on public affairs. Peter L. Berger, *Pyramids of Sacrifice* (New York: Basic Books, 1974) looks at the human cost of economic development, makes a critique of both capitalism and socialism, and attempts to formulate a political ethic adequate to the times. In *The Politics of Jesus* (Grand

Rapids: Wm. B. Eerdmans, 1972), John H. Yoder concludes that nonviolence lies at the heart of the political ethic of the New Testament. Paul Ramsey, *War and the Christian Conscience* (Durham: Duke University Press, 1961) is a classic treatment of Christian attitudes toward war.

Index